As I sing this song here with you I can not help shedding tears. I have never sung it before except as I stood looking upon the little child and praying for it in my heart. There is no little child here, but you are writing all these things down that they may not be lost and that our children may know what their fathers believed and practiced in this ceremony. So, as I sing, I am calling to Tiráwa atius to send down his breath upon you, to give you strength and long life. I am praying for you with all my spirit.

TAHIRUSSAWICHI
Native Keeper of Sacred Rites

AMERICAN INDIAN POETRY

AN ANTHOLOGY OF SONGS

AND CHANTS

EDITED BY GEORGE W. CRONYN

FOREWORD BY KENNETH LINCOLN

INTRODUCTION BY MARY AUSTIN

FAWCETT COLUMBINE · NEW YORK

A Fawcett Columbine Book
Published by Ballantine Books
Foreword copyright © 1991 by Kenneth Lincoln
Copyright © 1918, 1934 by George W. Cronyn
Copyright renewed 1962 by George W. Cronyn

Library of Congress Catalog Card Number: 73-133483
ISBN: 0-449-90670-1

Text design by Holly Johnson
Cover painting by Robert Freeman
Cover design by James R. Harris

Manufactured in the United States of America
First Ballantine Books Trade Edition: September 1991

10 9 8 7 6 5

ACKNOWLEDGMENTS

To *Poetry, a Magazine of Verse*, for permission to reprint "Early Moon," by Carl Sandburg; "Along the South Star Trail," "Sa-a Narai," and "On the Warpath," by Dr. Frank S. Gordon; "Listening," "Buffalo Dance," "Where the Fight Was," "The Wind," "Courtship," and "Parting," by Alice Corbin; "Neither Spirit nor Bird," and "Prayer to the Mountain Spirit," by Mary Austin; "Summer Dawn," "Song of the Search," "Song of the Whip-Plaiting," "Song of the Young Mother," "Change-Song," "Spring to the Earth-Witch," and "Chief Capilano Greets His Namesake at Dawn," by Constance Lindsay Skinner.

To the following magazines for permission to reprint interpretations by Constance Lindsay Skinner: *Scribner's Magazine*, "Wild Woman's Lullaby"; *Sunset Magazine*, "Lover's Hymn"; *The Delineator*, "Autumn Dawn"; *Others Magazine*, "Song of Basket Weaving." Miss Skinner also contributed "The Bilqula Death Song" and "Three Songs from the Haida." For additional work by Mary Austin, permission to reprint was granted by *McClure's Magazine*, "Song of the Hills"; *The Forum Magazine*, "Indian Songs"; *Everybody's*, "Medicine Songs."

The "Songs of the Yuma," by J. P. Harrington; the Chinook Eskimo, Kwa-kiutl Songs by Franz Boas; the Navajo Gambling Songs and "The Songs in the Garden of the House of God," by Washington Matthews, are reprinted by permission from the *Journal of American Folk Lore*. "Micmac War Songs" by S. T. Rand, and "Ojibwa Songs" by H. H. Schoolcraft and Charles Fenno Hoffman are reprinted from these authors' published volumes. The "Abanaki Songs" by John Reade appeared in the *Transactions of the Royal Society of Canada*. "The Lost Lagoon," and "The Song My Paddle Sings," by Pauline Johnson, are reprinted by permission of the Musson Book Co., Toronto. Permission was obtained from Little, Brown & Co. to reprint "Four Spirit Songs from California," translated by Jeremiah Curtin.

"The Haida Songs" by J. R. Swanton, are from publications of the American Ethnological Society. Space does not permit the publishers to present "The Hako: A Pawnee Ceremony," by Alice Fletcher, in full. It will be found in its complete form in the Twenty-Second Annual Report, Bureau of Ethnology, Smithsonian Institution. The translations by Natalie Curtis are reprinted by permission of Harper & Bros. from *The Indians' Book*, recommended to the reader for its intensive study of Indian songs and their sources.

From *Poetry, a Magazine of Verse*, came the inspiration for this anthology; the editor is grateful, also, to its generous contributors for many interpretations. Unless otherwise specified, all translations are from bulletins or reports of the Bureau of Ethnology, Smithsonian Institution, members of whose staff were most helpful . . .

DEDICATION

To those who have labored faithfully in the collection and transcription of the Art Forms of a Vanishing Race this book is respectfully dedicated.

Many of the songs and chants herein translated are very ancient; a number are modern, but none exhibit the slightest traces of European influence; they are genuine American Classics.

American Indian Poetry is no mere collection of literary curiosities; it is the intimate thought and soul of entire tribes of people revealed through their most personal medium—the song.

CONTENTS

SONGS FROM CALIFORNIA

SONGS FROM THE NORTHWEST COAST

SONGS FROM THE FAR NORTH

INTERPRETATIONS

CONSTANCE LINDSAY SKINNER

EARLY MOON

The baby moon, a canoe, a silver papoose canoe, sails and sails
    in the Indian West.

A ring of silver foxes, a mist of silver foxes, sit and sit around
    the Indian moon.

One yellow star for a runner, and rows of blue stars for more
    runners, keep a line of watchers.

O foxes, baby moon, runners, you are the panel of memory,
    fire-white writing tonight of the Red Man's dreams.

Who squats, legs crossed, and arms folded, matching its look
    against the moon-face, the star-faces, of the West?

Who are the Mississippi Valley ghosts, of copper foreheads, rid-
    ing wiry ponies in the night?—no bridles, love arms on the
    pony necks, riding in the night, a long old trail?

Why do they always come back when the silver foxes sit around
    the early moon, a silver papoose, in the Indian West?

FOREWORD

There died a myriad,
And of the best, among them,
For an old bitch gone in the teeth,
For a botched civilization, . . .
    E Z R A P O U N D,
        "Hugh Selwyn Mauberley"

The war was over. Eight and one-half million men lay dead in
trenches. The imperial West had blown and scrapped itself to
a wasteland. In this nadir of 1918 George W. Cronyn found an
alternative to the devastation. He turned to "Indian" transliter-
ations from Bureau of American Ethnology reports and anthol-
ogized them within a collection first called *The Path on the
Rainbow*. He borrowed the anthology's title from healing
Navajo "night chants," originally translated by Washington
Matthews, the cowboy surgeon:

> In Kinináeki.
> In the house made of dawn.
> In the story made of dawn.
> On the trail of dawn.
> O, Talking God! . . .
> From the base of the east.
> From the base of the Pelado Peak.
> From the house made of mirage,
> From the story made of mirage,
> From the doorway of rainbow,
> The path out of which is the rainbow. . . .

Cronyn's sampler of native literary wares was the first major collection to make headlines. Daniel Brinton's "Aboriginal American Authors and Their Productions" of 1883 lay stranded in academia, and Natalie Burlin Curtis's ethnomusicology in *The Indians' Book* of 1907 got far less press, though Theodore Roosevelt wrote from the White House in longhand as a frontispiece: "These songs cast a wholly new light—on the depth and dignity of Indian thought, the simple beauty and strange charm—the dream of a vanished elder world—of Indian poetry."

Why Indians in 1918? Tens of thousands of American Indians had volunteered for the First World War, though they were not even U.S. citizens. In fact, the United States government had declared war on many of their mothers and fathers from 1860 to 1890, when the Census Bureau finally verified that the frontier was closed. Congress granted all "Indians" dual citizenship in 1924 because of their native loyalty, making them "American" Indians in Buffalo Bill Cody's Wild West billing: that is, both ethnic aboriginals, among some five hundred (legally speaking) "domestic dependent nations," and "native" Americans, taxpaying veterans to be exact.

But what landed Cronyn's anthology at the eclectic threshold of Western literature? Indeed, how did *The Path on the Rainbow* eventually take the position of lead text in Jorge Luis Borges's classes on the American canon? Why culturally include, rather than exclude in the old frontier way, some four million pre-Columbian "Americans" who had been decimated, along with a few hundred remaining bison, to a quarter of a million political refugees in 1900? Xenophobia, racism, and genocide festered in the West on the flip side of the Buffalo Head nickel, when such a cultural scion as Frederic Remington himself could snarl, "Jews, Injuns, Chinamen, Italians, Huns," echoing Chivington and Custer, "the rubbish of the earth I hate." Indians had been made prisoners-of-war on reservations from the 1880s on—stripped of their clothing and culture and spirits by grizzled Civil War colonels, hardpan pioneers, make-over missionaries, sleazy traders, and hardass bureaucrats. These patriots figured that the only "good" Indians left (better dead than red) better get civilized, fast, before they disappeared. "The Indians must conform to 'the white man's ways,'" the Commissioner of Indian Affairs menaced in 1889, "peaceably if they will, forcibly if they must. . . . This civilization may not be the best possible, but it is the best the Indian can get." Listen up, pilgrims. When Edward Sheriff Curtis began catching their photographic "shadows" by the end of the century, he saw them as "vanishing" Americans.

Sorely, to be sure, the West needed a revised myth to supersede New World carte blanche (those who got the largesse of gold, land, power, and trade didn't want it taken back). So in a curious turnabout, the mythographers reached into the presence of the past and reinvented the Indian at the heart of this continent's humanity. The resurrected noble savage, reduced by a factor of sixteen since 1492, would rise above the ruins of anarchic Manifest Destiny on literary wings.

"From *Poetry, a Magazine of Verse*," Cronyn acknowledged, "came the inspiration for this anthology." These "genuine American classics," freely adapted not as translations but "interpretations" elsewhere *(McClure's, Scribner's, Sunset, Others)* by such as Carl Sandburg, Lew Sarett, and Amy Lowell, were grazed into rebirth by the February, 1917 "Aboriginal" issue of the country's premier poetry journal. "Suspicion arises definitely that the Red Man and his children," Sandburg tweaked readers in his praise of Frances Densmore's ethnomusicology, "committed direct plagiarisms on the modern imagists and vorticists." Ezra Pound published three of his early cantos and a review of T. S. Eliot's "The Love Song of J. Alfred Prufrock" in the August, 1917 *Poetry*, and Wallace Stevens printed "The Anecdote of the Jar" in the January, 1920 issue under the mock Victorian heading, "Pecksniffiana":

> The wilderness rose up to it.
> And sprawled around, no longer wild.
> The jar was round upon the ground
> And tall and of a port of air.

Further inspired by Cronyn's *The Path on the Rainbow*, Harriet Monroe in 1920 gathered yet another "aboriginal number" of *Poetry*, where Mary Austin and company personally revised nativist verse. Emma Hawkridge waxed neoprimitive in "The Painted Desert":

> Over the wasteland a strong wind goes;
> Like captured heat lies the cactus rose.
> The desert sings . . .

Whose paint, which rose? The next year Pablo Picasso and Wyndham Lewis sketched petroglyphic abstractions in *The Dial* (July, 1921), while D. H. Lawrence, newly relocating to the New World (now buried above Taos), confessed his anglophilic pettiness in "Snake." W. C. Williams scratched an American verse speech from what T. S. Eliot otherwise called, after Mallarme on Poe, "the language of the tribe," and W. B. Yeats celebrated an Irish tribal renaissance in early chapters from his *Autobiography*. Ethnographic reviews by Edward Sapir on Max Müller and Mary Austin on Frank Cushing underscored what Austin, midwife to Native American "re-expressions," then termed "the search for native sources of inspiration in the poetry and drama and design of Amerind art." Plumbing "deep-rooted aboriginal stock" and the very rhythms of the land itself, Austin would grouse in "Aboriginal American Literature" that "it is still easier to know more of Beowulf than of the Red Score of the Delaware, more of Homer than of the Creation Myth of the Zuñi, more of Icelandic sagas than of the hero myths of Iroquois and Navajo." Her point still stands.

Cronyn's sources had been the field work of Franz Boas, Daniel Brinton, Natalie Curtis Burlin, Frances Densmore, J. W. Fewkes, Alice Fletcher, John Peabody Harrington, James Mooney, Washington Matthews, H. H. Schoolcraft, Stephen Riggs, John R. Swanton, and other pioneering linguistic anthropologists godfathered by European-trained social scientists. Ruth Benedict, Ruth Bunzel, Ella Deloria, Charles Eastman, Francis La Flésche, Pliny Goddard, A. L. Kroeber, Robert Lowie, Elsie

Parsons, Archie Phinney, Paul Radin, Knud Rasmussen, Edward
Sapir, Frank G. Speck, Herbert Spindon, Ruth Underhill,
J. R. Walker, Clark Wissler, and scores of others would add
their translative genius to the field of American Indian Studies.
They would today lead to such contemporary Native American
writers as Paula Gunn Allen (Laguna Pueblo), Jim Barnes
(Choctaw), Diane Burns (Chippewa), Louise Erdrich (Chip-
pewa), Hanay Geiogamah (Kiowa), Joy Harjo (Creek), Linda
Hogan (Chickasaw), N. Scott Momaday (Kiowa), nila northSun
(Navajo), Simon Ortiz (Acoma Pueblo), Wendy Rose (Miwok-
Hopi), Leslie Silko (Laguna Pueblo), Mary TallMountain (Inuit),
Luci Tapahonso (Navajo), James Welch (Blackfeet-Gros Ventre),
Roberta Whiteman (Oneida), and Ray Young Bear (Mesquaki),
among several hundred more visible writers.

In her introduction to *The Path on the Rainbow* Austin
spoke of Americans instinctively seeking "a deeper footing in
their native soil." As a kind of New World neoclassicism—
grounded in Native American cultural bedrock—she appealed
to a sense of "the resident genius" of the native cultural ter-
rain, the pre-Columbian literary landscape. Here Americans
would find their own Homer, Plato, Diogenes, Sappho, Dido,
and Demeter in the tribal epics, philosophic parables, trick-
ster picaresques, grand satires, heroic romances, and creation
myths of some five hundred Native American cultures. Fran-
ces Densmore's translations were among the most moving ex-
amples:

> Soldiers,
>   you fled.
> Even the eagle dies.
>   LAKOTA

> The bush is sitting
>   under a tree
> and singing.
>   YUMAN

The water bug
is drawing
the shadows of the evening
toward him on the water.

YAQUI

In *Papago Music* Densmore recorded the "Song of Owl Woman,"
a shaman, and later raised the ticklish issue of re-creative trans-
lation: "The word 'rattling' was said to be a literal translation.
To us the word means simply a noise, which darkness could
scarcely make, but the sound of a rattle is associated with magic
and mystery in the mind of the Indian. When the poem is quoted
in this anthology the word 'rustling' is used instead, but this is
gentle and soft in its implication, and there is no vigor in the
corresponding verb. This is the song of a terrified spirit, facing
the greatest mystery that the mind can conceive. The subject is
worthy of Dante. In the 'great night' the spirit heard sounds of
fearful and stupendous import. The darkness 'came rattling.' "
The Path on the Rainbow renders it thus:

In the great night my heart will go out;
Toward me the darkness comes rustling.
In the great night my heart will go out.

PAPAGO

What is the difference between "rustling" and "rattling" dark-
ness? Which would Owl Woman choose, were she bilingual and
gifted with a poet's ear in both languages? What works better
in English? Which audience must a translation satisfy? What
kind of medicine does the chant work in either culture? If Dens-
more stays true to the Papago and betrays the poem's generative
spark in English, the translation fails as a poem. If she freely
adapts in the second tongue, the "poem" no longer speaks from
or for its source, but plays Indian. Can there be an authentic
crossing?

"The poem's form is the sound it makes when spoken,"

H. S. McAllister suggests. The further question of aesthetic form comes up in Densmore's translation of Sitting Bull's "last" song:

> A warrior
> I have been;
> now
> it is all over.
> A hard time
> I have.
>
> SONG OF SITTING BULL

What was the original "song"—singing for power, as Ruth Underhill titled her Papago collection—unrecorded by Tatanka Iyontake ("Bull Sitting" in Lakota, a mystic name from the four ages of human life)? Used-as-a-Shield told Densmore at Standing Rock in 1914, twenty-four years after the martyr's assassination, that he heard his Hunkpapa *wicasa wakañ* or "man holy," also a military genius, also a great healer, speaker, and singer with a high tenor voice, chant the song through the 1880s. What did it sound like? Densmore's musicology scores the key in E-flat minor with a descending fourth and two cascading thirds— something like a prophetic meadowlark's song (Sitting Bull's oracle bird, the Western meadowlark, warned him from childhood of danger).

> *I-ki-ci-ze wa-oñ koñ* he
> *wa-na he-ná-la ye-lo* he
> *i-yo-ti-ye ki-ya wa-oñ*

The first Lakota word means "head warrior" (confronting face-to-face) and the second "to know how," the third "to want." Occurring twice at the ends of lines, "he" is a vocable. *Wa-na* is "now" and *he-ná-la* means "all gone," terminated with the stress particle *ye-lo*. The long verb with its auxiliary ("make to be") in the third line means "to suffer, to find it hard," literally "to crash against." The last word, *wa-oñ*, means again "to know how," as in the opening line—and the nickname for a bear derives from it, *waoňze* (bears are known among the Lakota to be wise healers and warriors who sing with powerful hearts).

So, how does Densmore translate all this? Literally. And what about form? Freely. And the vocables? Untranslatable. The original? Each line rides on eight syllables—could they be syllabically musical? Most telling, can we sing Densmore's translation in the original musicology, as transcribed? Hardly. Perhaps this eight-syllable triad sounds better and better approximates the original:

> So I have been a warrior
> And now it is all over so
> I know to bear against hard times.

As Dell Hymes argues *("In Vain I Tried to Tell You")*, we may have to translate everything all over again, once the bilingual model is accepted and social scientists learn from verbal artists how to distinguish a verse line from a stump.

By 1929 Dorothy Demetracopoulou was collecting Dream Dance songs among the California Wintu around Mt. Lassen. "I recorded them intermittently," she wrote in *Anthropos* (1935), "chiefly as an expression of literary art, partly for their ethnographic value, partly for linguistic purposes. I secured them in text and translated them as literally as the discrepancy between Wintu and English would permit." Sadie Marsh lost her best friend, "who a little after came to her in a dream with a company of other female spirits, weeping, dancing, and singing this song":

> Down west, down west we dance,
> We spirits dance,
> We spirits weeping dance.

And the traditional Anonymous sang these translative pearls:

> Where will you and I sleep?
> At the down-turned jagged rim of the sky you
> and I will sleep.

Hymes asked in 1981, "Do these texts, restored to something like their true form, have power to move us, as part of the first literature of our land?"

Something has been moving Westerners toward American Indians for a long time now. Since the Renaissance, Europeans have shared American fascinations with the "native" American as the newest and oldest, most "free" and mostly "wild" peoples of the New World. It is as though a native Adam and Eve reappeared for a second chance in the Garden. D. H. Lawrence came down west with his runaway German wife, Frieda, to New Mexico in the 1920s, where they relocated among Pueblo Indians around Taos. It was a postwar move emblematic of Euroamerican migrations to the New World for three centuries. This godson of Raleigh returned to Italy, where Amerigo Vespucci was commissioned by the Medici to exploit the green breast of the Garden. Lawrence published *The Plumed Serpent* and *Mornings in Mexico* about "Indianizing" or Americanizing the White Man, in the wake of Cronyn's *The Path on the Rainbow*, and died before he could complete his writings on the original Americans. His ashes lie next to Frieda's in the Sangre de Cristo mountains today.

Thoreau died whispering "Indians" and "buffalo," they say, before he too could finish his masterwork on American natives. He left twelve cryptic notebooks in code. Walt Whitman worked in the Bureau of Indian Affairs in 1864, and Marianne Moore taught four years at Carlisle Indian School while Jim Thorpe was a student there. Isak Dinesen's father lived in Wisconsin in 1872 among *"les sauvages,"* as he called them, and she moved to Africa to find a native home. Ezra Pound, W. C. Williams, H. D., and the Imagists refashioned American Indian visual and verbal arts via *Poetry Magazine* and *The Dial*, through the translative insistences of Mary Austin and compatriot anthropologists, budding students of Franz Boas. This modernist neoprimitivism capped four centuries of Western organic thinking, as Diane and Jerome Rothenberg document in *Symposium of the Whole* (1983). Such neoprimitivism, in fact, was registered early this century among the Fauvists in France, the short-lived Vorticist movement of Pound and others in England, Picasso's prodigious wonder over native African masks ("Les Demoiselles D'Avignon" in 1907, for example, and 18,000-year-old cave paintings discovered in southern France). T. S. Eliot salvaged his *Waste Land* from these runes and ethnological models, via Frazer's *The Golden Bough*, Weston's grail mythology within a regenerate Christianity, and the linguistic anthropology coming from Europe by way of Boas, Sapir, and others.

In short, the "primitive" or "native" concerns of modernist rethinking, particularly in the arts and social sciences around the First World War, can be focused in discussions about the American Indian as cultured wild man. The speeches and oratory in Peter Nabokov's *Native American Testimony* remind us that the first recorded "American chronicles," as Constance Rourke noted, took place among Red-White ceremonies where the New World made treaties "at the forest's edge" with resident native nations. "By what names are they distinguished," Roger Williams catalogued in the 1643 *A Key into the Languages of America*: "First, those of the *English* giving: as *Natives, Salvages, Indians, Wild-men*, (so the *Dutch* call them *Wilden*), *Abergeny men, Pagans, Barbarians, Heathen*." Caliban, a name corrupted from *Carib* and *Khan* and *Canis* and "cannibal" (signifying to Columbus, it would seem, a dog-headed emperoraboriginal gorging on human flesh), has long been a symbol of native nobility and concomitant savagery, from Montaigne writing on misconceived cannibals, to Shakespeare's Prospero as the shamanic artist-surrogate of the Renaissance, to Rousseau's noble jungle savage, to Robert Penn Warren's American epic *Chief Joseph of the Nez Perce* in 1982, when he was appointed America's first poet laureate. Prospero adopts the wild man as his bestial son, and in so doing echoes cultural cataclysms first superimposed on the Brazilian Tupinamba, carried forward today: "this thing of darkness I / acknowledge mine" (*The Tempest* 5.1.275–76).

Rousseau and ensuing cultural romantics, Schiller, Schlegl, and Coleridge among them, godfathered native visionaries in America, from Cooper to Thoreau and Whitman, on to Hemingway, Snyder, Creeley, and Bly, among many others. These have artistic compatriots in Europe, from Gauguin in the riotous jungle, to Gaudier-Breska sculpting primal animal forms, to Stravinsky drumming the rites of spring, to Jawlensky painting Inuit and Hopi masks, to Miro's childlike play. Kafka sparked his "wish to become a Red Indian" in the unfinished *Amerika* of 1927: "If one were only an Indian, instantly alert, and on a racing horse, leaning against the wind, kept on quivering briefly over the quivering ground." In 1970 at UC Berkeley, recalls the Irish poet Seamus Heaney, now holding a Harvard chair, "There was a strong sense of contemporary American poetry in the West with Robert Duncan and Bly and Gary Snyder rejecting the intellectual, ironical, sociological idiom of poetry and going for the mythological. I mean everyone wanted to be a Red Indian, basically" (1979 *Ploughshares* interview).

"Know then," Johann Herder wrote a friend at the end of the eighteenth century, "the more alive and freedom-loving a people is . . . the more savage, that is, alive, free, sensuous, lyrically active, its songs must be." Cronyn caught the drift in Densmore's Chippewa translation:

> As my eyes
> search
> the prairie
> I feel the summer in the spring.

Puccini went so far as to write an opera with an Indian chorus in 1910, *La Fanciulla del West*, "The Golden Girl of the West," featuring a female Indian chorus. A Prussian convict, Karl May, wrote perhaps the most widely read "Indian" fiction in the world—about the noble Winnetou and his Caucasian companion, Old Shatterhand—and it competed with Longfellow's Hiawatha and Cooper's Leatherstocking tales for top Indianist billing abroad. Karl May was the favorite author of no less than Karl Marx, Bertolt Brecht, Adolf Hitler, and Albert Schweitzer. Finally, Dylan Thomas acted out the "Red Man" myth of the wild child at home in Wales in "the Gorsehill jungle" of *Por-*

trait of the Artist as a Young Dog: "On my haunches, eager and alone, casting an ebony shadow, with the Gorsehill jungle swarming, the violent, impossible birds and fishes leaping, hidden under four-stemmed flowers the height of horses, in the early evening in a dingle near Carmarthen, my friend Jack Williams invisibly near me, I felt all my young body like an excited animal surrounding me. . . . There, playing Indians in the evening, I was aware of me myself in the exact middle of a living story, and my body was my adventure and my name."

The Path on the Rainbow would spawn Margot Astrov's *The Winged Serpent* at the end of the Second World War, both poetry and prose culled from B.A.E. reports of the 1880s through the 1930s, with snippets of contextual notes and a serviceable introduction. In a Stanford dissertation published under the title *The Sky Clears* (1951), A. Grove Day collected even newer materials under Yvor Winters, who went on to tutor Scott Momaday to stardom (one of the five best poets to write a great poem in the American language, Winters thundered in *Forms of Discovery*). Day's monograph was a step toward an emerging bicultural sense of native poetics.

By the end of the 1960s, Indian anthologies were popping up like wildflowers: Jerome Rothenberg's inventive *Shaking the Pumpkin*, William Brandon's a bit too freely reworked *The Magic World*, John Bierhorst's pellucid *In the Trail of the Wind*, Robert Dodge and Joseph McCullough's contemporary *Voices from Wah'Kon-Tah* and the newer Indian writers in Dick Lourie's *Come to Power*, Duane Niatum's *Carriers of the Dream Wheel*, and Shirley Hill Witt and Stan Steiner's *The Way*. Brian Swann's *Song of the Sky* (1985) "re-expressed" native song-poems improvisationally, "shadows of shadows," à la Nancy Curtis, and brought the translative cycle full circle. Geronimo, the Apache warrior in his 70s, told Nancy Curtis: "The song that I will sing is an old song, so old that none knows who made it. . . . The song tells how, as I sing, I go through the air to a holy place where Yusan (the Supreme Being) will give me power to do wonderful things. I am surrounded by little clouds, and as I go through the air I change, becoming spirit only."

>   through the air
>   as I move
>   changing
>   I go to   a sacred place
>   this is the way
>   going up
>   little cloud   me

If our *first* literatures are native, and our translations echo
old worlds colliding with new ones, the "power to move us"
still resides in George W. Cronyn's *American Indian Poetry*.
Read it well. It serves as a cornerstone to our multicultural di-
versity and ancient rootedness in this good land.

>   K E N N E T H   L I N C O L N
>   *Professor of English and*
>   *American Indian Studies, UCLA*

Kenneth Lincoln was born in Texas and grew up in northwest Nebraska where his great-grandparents homesteaded along the North Platte River and ranching sand-hills. He graduated from public high school in Alliance, Nebraska, a cattle and farming town south of Wounded Knee on the Pine Ridge Sioux Reservation. Lincoln was adopted into the Oglala Sioux by the Mark Monroe family and given the Lakota name, *Mato Yamni*. He went to Stanford University for an B.A. in American Literature, to Indiana University for a Ph.D. in British Literature, and to UCLA in 1969, where he teaches Modern and Native American Literatures. Kenneth Lincoln has developed American Indian Studies curricula, published widely in the field— *Native American Renaissance* (University of California Press, 1983), *The Good Red Road* (Harper & Row, 1987), UCLA Native American Poetry Series (1975–1991)— and chaired the country's first interdisciplinary Master's Program in American Indian Studies. Oxford University Press will publish his *Indi'n Humor: Bicultural Play in Native America* in 1992.

INTRODUCTION

The poetic faculty is, of all man's modes, the most responsive to natural environment, the most sensitive and the truest record of his reactions to its skyey influences, its floods, forests, morning colors. It is the first to register the rise of his spirits to the stimulus of new national ideals. If this were not so there would be no such thing as nationality in art, and it is only by establishing some continuity with the earliest instances of such reaction that we can be at all sure that American poetic genius has struck its native note. Therefore it becomes appropriate and important that this collection of American Indian verse should be brought to public notice at a time when the whole instinctive movement of the American people is for a deeper footing in their native soil. It is the certificate of our adoption, that the young genius of our time should strike all unconsciously on this ancient track to the High Places.

Poetic art in America, at the time it began to be overlaid by European culture, had reached a mark close to that of the Greeks at the beginning of the Homeric era. The lyric was well developed, the epic was nascent, and the drama was still in the Satyris stage of development, a rude dance ritual about an altar or a sacrificial fire. Neither poetry nor drama were yet divorced from singing, and all art was but half-born out of the Great Mystery. Magic was sung, and songs had magic power. Both were accompanied by appropriate bodily movement, so that an Indian will say indifferently, I cannot sing that dance, or I cannot dance that song. Words, melody and movement were as much mixed as the water of a river with its own ripples and its rate of flowing. Hum a few bars of a plainsman's familiar song, and he will say, puzzled, "It ought to be a war song," but without the words he will scarcely identify it. Words may become obsolete so that the song is untranslatable, but so long as enough of it remains to hold together the primary emotional impulse out of which it sprang, the Indian finds it worthy to be sung. He is, indeed, of the opinion that "White man's songs, they talk too much."

This partly explains why most Indian songs are songs for occasions. The rest of the explanation lies in the fact that songs have magic power. Tiráwa, Wokonda, The Friend of the Soul of Man, is in everything; in the field we plant, the stone we grind with, the bear we kill. By singing, the soul of the singer is put in harmony with the essential Essence of Things. There are songs for every possible adventure of tribal life; songs for setting out on a journey, a song for the first sight of your destination, and a song to be sung by your wife for your safe return. Many of these songs occur detached from everything but the occasion from which they sprang, such as the women's grinding song, measured to the *plump, plump*! of the mealing stone, or the Paddle Song which follows the swift rhythm of the stroke. Others, less descriptive and retaining always something of a sacred character, occur originally as numbers in the song sequences by which are celebrated the tribal Mysteries.

Back of every Indian ceremony lies a story, the high moments of which are caught up in song, while the burden of the narrative is carried by symbolic rite and dance. The unequal social development of contemporaneous tribes affords examples from every phase of structural development from the elemental dance punctuated by singing exclamations to the Mountain Chant of the Zuñi in which the weight of the story has broken down the verse variants into strong simple forms capable of being carried in a single memory. Halfway between them is the ritual sequence of the Midéwan.

The practical necessity of being preserved and handed on by word of mouth only, must be constantly borne in mind in considering the development of Indian verse forms.

It operated to keep the poetry tied to its twin-born melody, which assisted memory, and was constantly at work modifying the native tendency to adjust the rhythm to every changing movement of the story. Ancient Chippeway singers kept ideographic birch bark memoranda of their songs, and wampum belts commemorated the events that gave use to them, but the songs themselves came down from their ancient sources hundreds of years in the stream of human memory shaped by its limitations.

From the Zuñi Creation Cycle with its sustained narrative style to the Homeric Epic is but one poetic bound, the space between them, represented in old world literature by the Norse Sagas and the Kalevala, indicated but not filled, in America, by prose relations. It is probable that if we had anything like adequate records of the literature of vanished tribes, this pre-Homeric period would show notable examples of epic stuff. Nobody really knows how the Walam Olum or the Creek Migration Myths were recited. They embodied whole epochs of tribal history, to which the known literary remains were merely the mnemonic key, a tally of significant items. In every tribe are floating songs which appear to be fragments from a story sequence the key of which has been lost, and it is not unlikely that records like the Red Score would have owned complete, if detached, narratives of the historic events so slightly indicated, some of which may yet yield themselves to the patient researcher.

For the casual reader more interest attaches to the personal songs, the lullabies, love songs, most of all the man's *own* song which he makes of his great moment. This is a peculiar personal possession. No one may sing it without his permission. He may bestow it on a friend, or bequeath it to the tribe on his death, but it is also possible that he may die without having sung it to anyone but his god.

On one occasion in the high Sierras I observed my Indian packer going apart at a certain hour each day to shuffle rhythmically with his feet and croon to himself. To my inquiry he said it was a song which he had made, to be sung by himself and his wife when they were apart from one another.

It had no words; it was just a song. Wherever they were they turned each in the direction he supposed the other to be, when the sun was a bow-shot above the edge of the heavens, and sang together. This is the sort of incident which gives the true value of song in aboriginal life. It is not the words which are potent, but the states of mind evoked by singing, states which the simple savage conceived as being supernally good for him. He evoked them therefore on all his most personal occasions. Poetry is the Path on the Rainbow by which the soul climbs; it lays hold on the Friend of the Soul of Man. Such exalted states are held to be protective and curative. Medicine men sing for their patients, and, in times of war, wives gather around the Chief's woman and sing for the success of their warriors.

"Calling on Zeus by the names of Victory" as Euripides puts it.

It is this inherent power of poetry to ·aise the psychic plane above the accidents of being, which gives meaning to the custom of the Death Song. As he sees his moment approaching, the Indian throws himself, by some profound instinct of self-preservation, into the highest frame of mind attainable. When men in battle broke into the death song, they had committed themselves to the last desperate adventure. Dying of enfeebling sickness, their friends came and sang around them. One such I heard, the death song of a Yokut Song Maker. It was very simple:

> "All my life
> I have been seeking,
> Seeking!"

What more than this have the schools taught us!

Of Indian meters there has been no competent study made. The whole problem of form is inextricably complicated with melody and movement. The necessity of making his verse conform to a dance, probably accounts for the liberal use of meaningless syllables. To our ear no specific forms seem indicated, yet that the Indians recognize a certain correspondence between form and meaning is certain. They will readily classify songs of other tribes in unknown tongues into songs of love or war or magic. The genius of the tribal language is a determining factor. No clumsiness of translation can quite disguise the—from our point of view—superior singableness of Chippeway verse. In general, poetry of forest dwellers is more lyric than the songs of mountain and mesa. An inquiry which I once made into the psychology of the Indian sign language with a view to discovering a possible relation between it and Greek manual gesture as displayed in ancient graphic art, led to the conclusion that Indian rhythms arise rather in the centre of self-preservation than of self-consciousness. Which is only another way of saying that poetry is valued primarily by the aboriginal for the reaction it produces within himself rather than for any effect he is able to produce on others by means of it. This is true even of that class of songs which originates wholly in the desire to affect the fortunes or well being of others, songs of healing and magic formulae.

The first stage of Indian magic is the rise of the singer on his own song to a plane of power; only while he is in this plane is he able to bring the wish of his client to pass. It is a natural process of deterioration which leads to the song being thought of as having potency in itself.

Magic songs can generally be recognized by the form of affirmation in which they are cast, as in the Winnebago Love Song, which is not really a song of love, but a song to secure success in love,

> Whosoe'r I look upon
> He becomes love crazed.

or the Cherokee formula to insure the constancy of the beloved, and the Micmac vengeance song

> Death I make,
> Singing

Among the Navajo the magic effect is made certain by the four-fold repetition of the affirming phrase, four being a sacred number.

These are all items which have to be taken into account in interpreting American Indian poetry. It is in the very nature of primitive verse that it should require interpretation, even among the audiences for whom it is originally intended. For verse is to the Red singer but a shorthand note to his emotions, a sentence or two, a phrase out of the heart of the situation. It is the "inside song" alone which is important. Says the Medicine Man, explaining these matters, "You see Injun man singin' an' cryin' while he sing. It ain't what he singin' make him cry; iss what the song make him think, thass what he cryin' about."

This inside song may be a fleeting instant of revelation, or a very long story . . . as if one should try in the Zuñi fashion to compress the whole Christian myth into one bitter cry,

> My God! My God!
> Why hast Thou deserted me?

> Hi-ihiya, naiho-o,
> It is finished,
> In beauty it is finished
> Nai-ho-o!

Whole cycles of tribal or personal experience can lie behind some such simple but absolute phrasing. It is this hidden beauty for which the interpreter must dig deep into aboriginal life.

The Ghost Dance songs included in this collection are scarcely intelligible until the reader realizes that they are supposed to be the flashes of revelation brought from the dead in dreams, foretelling the approach of a spiritual revival.

Thus it came to the Cheyenne:

> I bring the whirlwind
> That you may know one another
> ⸻
> We shall live again!

To the Piaute also

> Fog, fog,
> Lightning, lightning,
> Whirlwind, whirlwind.

and then

> The cottonwoods are growing tall
> They are growing tall and green.

For to the Piaute from his flat Reservation on Walker River, the faint young green of the cottonwoods is the first sign of that new growth which follows after seasonal storms. Any adequate rendering of these songs would have to convey in native figures all this sense of immanent world-overturning and spiritual reëstablishment in the Oneness of God and the Brotherhood of man.

> (It is I who wear the Morning Star on my forehead . . .
> All that grows upon the earth is mine
> Says the Father.)

Thus interpreted they would rank with the prophetic utterances of the herdsman of Tekoa. It is quite possible, indeed, that in time all these ghostly songs would have been detached from their obscure authors and ascribed to the Messiah of the Ghost Dance, who would have been reckoned among the major prophets.

For such illuminating gleams that Indian poetry can throw on the genesis of inspired literature, its study would be worthwhile, even if without the renewal of our native stock of poetic forms and figures.

It is probable that the best Indian poetry has been lost to us in the stamping out of superior tribes.

This would be particularly the case in the south, where

social development had reached a stage which only the pueblos and the Five Nations of western New York approached.

Miss Convers has shown us in the fragments of Iroquois ritual something of what might still be recovered from the remnants of that race, but this single example from the forgotten tribe of Tenasa, on the shore of the Missi-sippu seems to me to overleap all time and space and touch the hidden source of Greek inspiration. It is a marriage song, the faithful translation of an unliterary explorer, Greek in its mode, and in a certain tender irony of mood, but with touches to which only a full knowledge of Indian thought can give their full value, for all of which I venture to give it the isolation of its native quality.

Tiakens, thou buildest a house,
Thou bringest a wife to live in it.

Thou art married, Tiakens, thou art married,
Thou wilt become famous, thy children wilt name thee among
   the elders.
Think of Tiakens as an old man!

By what name is thy bride known,
Is she beautiful?
Are her eyes soft as the light of the moon?
Is she a strong woman?
Didst thou understand her signs as she danced
        to thee?
I know not whether thou lovest her,
    Tiakens,
What saidst the old man, her father, when you asked for his
   pretty daughter?
What betrothal gifts didst thou give her?

Rejoice, Tiakens, be glad, be happy,
Build thyself a happy home.
This is the song of its building.

The single line which identifies the song of Tiakens as intrinsically American is that one which inquires:

Didst thou understand her signs when she danced to thee? embodying as it does a very widespread aboriginal belief that in the dance and song, more than in any other medium, a maiden revealed the physical capacity and the power of sustained emotion which fitted her for marriage. Since when, and with what unhappy results, have *we* forgotten that creative emotion is a qualification for marriage! We do shallowly indeed when we dismiss the dance and song as mere millinery of courtship. They are the speech of the spirit identifying itself with cosmic forces. I do not know whether or not the Tenasa had the custom known on the Pacific Coast as the Dance of Marriageable Maidens, but I know that if you cut deeply into any Indian poem it yields that profound and palpitant humanism without which no literary art can endure.

Failure to realize the living background of Indian art has led to singular misinterpretation, in a class of songs common to every tribe, and almost invariably translated as love songs by the novice. These are the songs of the Mystics, Songs of Seeking. They record the unavailing search of the soul for the Absolute, for touch of that Great Mystery which is the object of the Indian's profoundest aspiration. Two such songs may be found in Frederick Burton's collection of Ojibway music, done into rather sentimental love ditties, the "Lake's Sheen" and the "Birch Bark Canoe," though their character as religious songs was so plainly marked that Mr. Burton himself commented on the singularity of Indian sweethearts forever getting themselves lost and requiring to be sought. It is well to remember before attempting the interpretation of an Indian love song, that the great Mystics have always appropriated the intimate language of the heart for the soul's quest. As will be seen from the examples which Mr. Cronyn has included in his collection, the work of interpreting our treasure of Indian verse has been but lightly begun. While some of these, notably Miss Corbin's "Across the River" leave nothing to be desired of the spirit, form and content of the original, many others have had frankly to sacrifice one of them.

In my own interpretations I have been feeling rather for a full expression of Indian thought, than for lyrical quality.

And in any case, mine is not a singing gift. All Indian verse is either sung or chanted, but the difficulty of fitting Indian rhythms to European music is only surpassed by the difficulty of getting Indian music arranged in European notation.

The long divided Muses of poetry, music and dance must come together again for the absolute rendering. Enough cannot be said in praise of the work of Miss Fletcher, Natalie Curtis, Frank Cushing and Washington Mathews, to mention no others, for the clarity and sincerity of their literal translations. The interpreter's work is all before him. I know of no task so salutory to the poet who would, first of all, put himself in touch with the resident genius of his own land.

MARY AUSTIN

SONGS FROM THE

EASTERN WOODLANDS

THE PARTED LOVERS
ABANAKI

I

THE MAN SINGS

My parents think they can separate me from the girl I love;
We have vowed to love each other while we live.
Their commands are vain: we shall see each other while the
    world lasts.
Yes! let them say or do what they like; we shall see each
    other while the rocks stand.

THE WOMAN SINGS

Here I sit on this point, whence I can see the man that I love.
Our people think that they can sever us; but I shall see him
    while the world lasts.
Here shall I remain, in sight of the one I love.

II

THE GIRL DESERTED BY HER JEALOUS COMPANIONS
SINGS

Now I am left on this lonely island to die—
No one to hear the sound of my voice.
Who will bury me when I die?
Who will sing my death-song?

My false friends leave me here to die alone;
Like a wild beast, I am left on this island to die.
I wish the wind spirit would carry my cry to my love!
My love is swift as the deer; he would speed through the
   forest to find me.
Now I am left on this lonely island to die.
I wish the wind spirit would carry my cry to my love!
My love is as swift as the deer; he would speed through the
   forest to find me;
Now I am left on this lonely island to die.
I wish the spirit of air would carry my breath to my love.
My love's canoe, like sunlight, would shoot through the water
   to my side;
But I am left on this lonely island to die, with no one to pity
   me but the little birds.
My love is brave and strong; but, when he hears my fate, his
   heart will break.
And I am on this lonely island to die.
Now the night comes on, and all is silent but the owl.
He sings a mournful song to his mate, in pity for me.
I will try to sleep.
I wish the night spirit to hear my song; he will tell my love of
   my fate; and when I awake, I shall see the one I love.
I am on this lonely island to die.

III

HER LOVER SEES HER IN A DREAM AND, GOING TO
SEARCH FOR HER, SINGS

Come, my beloved, let us go up that shining mountain, and
   sit together on that shining mountain; there we will watch
   the Sun go down in beauty from that shining place.
There we will sit, till the Night Traveler arises in beauty
   about the shining mountain; we will watch him as he
   climbs to the beautiful skies.

We will also watch the little Stars following their chief.

We will also watch the Northern Lights playing their game of ball in their cold, glistening country.

There we will sit, on the beautiful mountain, and listen to the Thunder beating his drum.

We will see the flashes from the lit pipe of the Lightning.

We will see the great Whirlwind race with Squall.

There we will sit, until all creatures drowse.

There we will hear the great Owl sing his usual song: "Go-to-sleep-all," and see all animals obey his call.

There we will sit in beauty on the mountain, and watch the small Stars in their sleepless flight.

They do not mind the song, "go-to-sleep-all"; neither will we mind it, but sit more closely together, and think of nothing but ourselves, on the beautiful mountain.

Again, the "go-to-sleep-all" will be heard, and the Night Traveler will come closer to warn us that all are sleeping, except ourselves and the little Stars.

They and their chief are coursing along, and our minds go with them.

Then the Owl sleeps; no more is heard "go - to - sleep - all"; the Lightnings flash afar; the great pipe is going out; the Thunder ceases beating his drum; and though our bodies urge us to be sleeping, we sit in beauty still upon the shining mountain.

VENGEANCE SONG
MICMAC

Death I make, singing
Heh-yeh! heh-yeh! heh-yeh! heh-yeh!
Bones I hack, singing
Heh-yeh! heh-yeh! heh-yeh! heh-yeh!
Death I make, singing!
Heh-yeh! heh-yeh! heh-yeh! heh-yeh!

IROQUOIS RITUAL OF FIRE AND DARKNESS

The members of the Ho-no-tci-no-ga Society assemble. Now the Medicine Doctor or Shaman casts the sacred tobacco on the medicine-blaze, and in a low voice he chants:

Great Spirit who puts us to sleep in darkness,
We thank thee for the silences of darkness.
(Singer)
Now I ask blessing and make prayers.
(He sprinkles sacred tobacco on the fire.
Then he speaks to the Invisible:)
Now I give you tobacco,
You, the great Darkness!
(To the Thunder Spirit)
Now we act as we offer you tobacco!
You love it most of all offerings.
With it you will hear us better
And not tire of our talking
But love us with all power
Beyond all treasures
Or spreading of words through the air!
All men traveling under great heaven
You have invited, your grandchildren and all nations;
Oh you, maker of noise,
You, the great Thunderer!
Your grandchildren wish to thank you!
All your grandchildren have asked me
To offer this tobacco upon the mountain to you!
(Speaking to the Great Spirit)
You the All-maker,
Above-all-high
Best Friend of people!
We ask you to help us!
We implore your favor!
I have spoken.

The lights are extinguished, leaving the assembly in total darkness.
The Watcher of the Medicine uncovers the bundles, exposing it to
the air, and as he does so a faint luminous cloud hovers over the
table and disappears. Now the Chanter gives the signal and the
members sing:

THE CHANT OF DARKNESS

> Wait here in the darkness!
> Come, all you who listen,
> Go the magic journey:
> Now the sky is empty
> Of all sun-and-star-shine;
> Come, we lose our footing.
> Night no friend of ours is;
> She has shut her eyelids.
> Moon who has forgotten
> Lets us wait in darkness!

Now the chiefs take their rattles, shaking them softly as the Chanter
sings and members of the clan give the whip-poor-will cry.

THE CHANT OF INVITATION TO THE WHIP-POOR-WILL
TOTEM

> *(Chorus)*
> Thus sings the Whip-poor-will,
> Follow me, follow me!
> Thus speaks the Chief to him,
> Yes, I will follow you!
> Lo! the night darkening
> Stalks through the shadow-land;
> No light to beckon us
> Murmurs the waterfall,
> Thus sings the river-voice!
> Someone is nearing us,

Creeping upon us close,
Two fires of eyes are close
Lighting the forest path—
Hear how his breath blows by!
Fol-low me, fol-low me,—
So sings the whip-poor-will!
Yes, I am following—
Thus the Chief answers him.

Cries announce that the Wolf and his mate have entered the room.

Hark the trees whispering
Bend their old bodies low,
Not the strong North Wind's hand
Nay, but One great and swift
Parts them with whistling breath!
Hark! how the thickets snap!
Fearless the footfalls pass
Pushing the trees apart!
Great horns dividing them.
(Again the Whip-poor-will chorus)

Now Buck and Doe, with cries, enter. The song continues:

How I go shivering!
No snow is falling now,
Where hides the sun his fire?
Something swift-footed comes
Roaring and warning me!
Eyes of the night it blinds,
Falling like heavy mist!
Now it creeps close to me,
Warning and beckoning
Where the black forest looms.
(Whip-poor-will chorus)

The Bear and his mate have come and the song goes on:

How the wind whistles now!
No one dares race with it.
Great trees bend low to it,
Rivers fight back to it,

Roaring and splashing it!
Hear how its strong wings beat
Deep in the gusty sky!
High through the night it flies
Whistling and screaming, still
Hunting the prey that runs!
(Whip-poor-will chorus)

The Hawk and its mate are announced. Then rites symbolizing the dangers of the forest tangles and swampy horrors are performed. According to the legend Eagle must dismiss the meeting. His coming, which is imitated on the small flute, announces the day. As the dawn-light penetrates the ceremonial place the last chorus is chanted of

THE EAGLE

Deep the dew-water falls
No one comes close to me!
Where are you, Whip-poor-will?
Why am I waiting now
Calling you, calling you?
Screaming the night away
With his great feathers spread
Catching the darkness up
I hear the Eagle-bird
Pulling the blanket back
From the east, sleeping still.
How swift he flies, bearing the sun to the morning;
See how he perches there on the trail of the east-sky.
Whip-poor-will, Whip-poor-will,
No more I follow thee!
When night springs up again
Will you cry, "Follow me?"

The singing ends and the matrons bring in food and distribute it to all.

FIRE-FLY SONG
OJIBWA

Flitting white-fire insects!
Wandering small-fire beasts!
Wave little stars about my bed!
Weave little stars into my sleep!
Come, little dancing white-fire bug,
Come, little flitting white-fire beast!
Light me with your white-flame magic,
Your little star-torch.

CALLING-ONE'S-OWN
OJIBWA

Awake ! flower of the forest, sky-treading bird of the prairie.
Awake ! awake ! wonderful fawn-eyed One.
When you look upon me I am satisfied; as flowers that drink
    dew.
The breath of your mouth is the fragrance of flowers in the
    morning,
Your breath is their fragrance at evening in the moon-of-
    fading-leaf.
Do not the red streams of my veins run toward you
As forest-streams to the sun in the moon of bright nights?
When you are beside me my heart sings; a branch it is,
    dancing,
Dancing before the Wind-spirit in the moon of strawberries.
When you frown upon me, beloved, my heart grows dark—
A shining river the shadows of clouds darken,
Then with your smiles comes the sun and makes to look like
    gold
Furrows the cold wind drew in the water's face.
Myself! behold me! blood of my beating heart.

Earth smiles—the waters smile—even the sky-of-clouds smiles—
    but I,
I lose the way of smiling when you are not near,
Awake ! awake ! my beloved.

OJIBWA WAR SONGS

I

Hear my voice, Birds of War!
I prepare a feast for you to feed on;
I see you cross the enemy's lines;
Like you I shall go.
I wish the swiftness of your wings;
I wish the vengeance of your claws;
I muster my friends;
I follow your flight.
Ho, you young men warriors,
Bear your angers to the place of fighting!

II

From the south they came, Birds of War—
Hark! to their passing scream.
I wish the body of the fiercest,
As swift, as cruel, as strong.
I cast my body to the chance of fighting.
Happy I shall be to lie in that place,
In that place where the fight was,
Beyond the enemy's line.

III

Here on my breast have I bled!
See—see! these are fighting-scars!
Mountains tremble at my yell!
I strike for life.

LOVE-SONG
WINNEBAGO

Whomsoe'er look I upon
    He becomes love-crazed;
Whomsoe'er speak I unto,
    He becomes love-crazed;
Whomsoe'er whisper I to,
    He becomes love-crazed;
All men who love women,
Them I rule, them I rule,
    My friend;
Whom I touch, whom I touch,
    He becomes love-crazed.

HOLY SONG
WINNEBAGO

(Saith the Spirit,
"Dream, oh, dream again,
And tell of me,
    Dream thou!")

Into solitude went I
And wisdom was revealed to me.
    (Saith the Spirit,
    "Dream, oh, dream again,
    And tell of me,
        Dream thou!")

Let the whole world hear me,
Wise am I!
    (Now saith the Spirit,
    "Tell of me,
        Dream thou!")

All was revealed to me;
From the beginning
Know I all, hear me!
All was revealed to me!
    (Now saith the Spirit,
    "Tell of me,
        Dream thou!")

SACRED MIDÉ SONGS
OJIBWA

Drifting snow,
    why do I sing?

The Sun and Moon,
Their bodies
    shine over the world
    unto me as unto you, my Midé
friend.

SONGS OF THE CHIPPEWA

HEALING SONG

They are in close consultation
    with their heads together
    Wenabojo
    and his grandmother.

LOVE-CHARM

What are you saying to me?
I am arrayed like the roses
    and beautiful as they.

I AM WALKING

Toward calm and shady places
I am walking
on the earth.

THEY THINK ME UNWORTHY

They think me unworthy
my Midé brethren
but look and see
the length of my wigwam.

THE SOUND IS FADING AWAY

The sound is fading away
It is of five sounds
freedom
The sound is fading away
It is of five sounds.

DOCTOR'S SONG

I am singing and dreaming in my poor way
over the earth
I who will again disembark
upon earth.

SONG OF THE TREES

The wind
only
I am afraid of.

SONG OF THE THUNDERS

Sometimes
     I go about pitying
     myself
     while I am carried by the wind
     across the sky.

THE APPROACH OF THE STORM

From the half
     of the sky
     that which lives there
     is coming, and makes a noise.

I AM AFRAID OF THE OWL

Very much
     also
     I
     of the owl
     am afraid
     whenever I am sitting alone
          in the wigwam.

I AM AS BRAVE AS OTHER MEN

Men who are brave and heroic
     as you esteem them to be
Like them
     I also
     consider myself to be.

MY MUSIC REACHES TO THE SKY

My music
reaches
to the sky.

FAREWELL TO THE WARRIORS

Come
it is time for you to depart
We are going on a long journey.

SONG OF THE MAN WHO WAS TO BE HUNG

The thunders will take me home,
whenever I mind to go home,
my friends,
and the wind
it will take me home, too.

FRIENDLY SONG

I

Over there
in the sky
they have taken pity on me.

II

The sky
loves to hear me.

GAMING SONG

I will go home
if I am beaten
after more articles
to wager.

WAR SONGS

At Co'goben's
    village
    they are weeping
    the men

At Co'goben's
    village
    they are wailing
    the women.

I feel no fear
    when the Great River man
    death
    speaks of.

THE MAN WHO STAYED HOME

Although
    Jinwábe
    considers himself
    a man
    his wife
    certainly
    takes all his attention.

ARROW SONG

Scarlet
    is its head

SONG OF THE BUFFALO

Strike ye
    our land
    with curved horns

SONG OF THE MINISINOWUCK

It is uncertain what will happen
        to the one from whom I fly
It is uncertain what will happen
        to the one from whom I rise.

DRUM SONG

I make them dance
        those brave men
    those brave men
        every one of them.

SONG OF WOMAN-OF-THE-RED-SKY, WHO WENT WITH HER HUSBAND, SINGING, INTO BATTLE

At that time
        if I had been a man
        truly
        a man
        I would have seized.

DEATH SONG OF NAMEBINES

The odor of death
I discern the odor of death
        in the front of my body.

THE SIOUX WOMEN GATHER UP THEIR WOUNDED

The Sioux women
        pass to and fro wailing
        as they gather up
        their wounded men
The voice of their weeping comes back
        to us.

THEY ARE PLAYING A GAME

The noise of passing feet
      on the prairie
They are playing a game as they come
      those men.

SCALP SONG

I wonder
      if she is humiliated
      the Sioux woman
      that I cut off her head.

SONG OF REJOICING

It shall be
      that I rejoice
O, my son
      your elder brother
      you have brought back
O, my son
      it shall be
      that I rejoice
O, my son.

DEATH SONG

Is there anyone who
      would weep for me?
My wife
      would weep for me.

SONG OF THE BUTTERFLY

In the coming heat
      of the day
      I stood there.

MAPLE SUGAR

Maple sugar
     is the only thing
     that satisfies me.

A SONG OF SPRING

As my eyes
     search
     the prairie
     I feel the summer in the spring.

CARRIED AROUND THE SKY

As the wind is carrying me
     around the sky.

THE SKY WILL RESOUND

It will resound finely
     the sky
     when I come making a noise.

AN OVERHANGING CLOUD

An overhanging
     cloud
     repeats my words with pleasing sound.

HEAPS OF CLOUDS

Great heaps
     of clouds
     in the direction I am looking.

THE NOISE OF THE VILLAGE

Whenever I pause
the noise
of the village.

MIDÉ BURIAL SONG

Neniwá
let us stand
and you shall see
my body
as I desire.

LOVE SONGS

MY LOVE HAS DEPARTED

I

A loon
I thought it was
but it was
my love's
splashing oar.

II

To Sault Ste. Marie
he has departed
My love has gone on before me,
Never again
can I see him.

THE GENEROUS ONE

Why should
I, even I

be jealous
because of that bad boy?

RECOVERY

Do not weep
I am not going to die.

LOVE-HURT

Although he said it
    still
I am filled with longing
when I think of him.

GLAD-PARTING

Come
    I am going away
I pray you
    let me go
I will soon return
Do not
    weep for me
Behold
    we will be very glad
    to meet each other
    when I return
Do not
    weep for me.

INVITATION

My sweetheart
    a long time
    I have been waiting for you

to come over
where I am.

YOU DESIRE VAINLY

You desire vainly
that I seek you
the reason is
I come
to see your younger sister.

HE IS GONE

I might grieve
I am sad
that he has gone
my lover.

SONG OF AN AMBITIOUS MOTHER

I am asking for
Bugac's
daughter
My big
brass kettle
he is giving.

NONSENSE SONG OF THE GAME OF SILENCE

(If you speak or laugh you are defeated)
It is hanging
in the edge of the sunshine
It is a pig I see
with its double (cloven) hoofs
It is a very fat pig.
The people who live in a hollow tree
are fighting

They are fighting bloodily
He is rich
He will carry a pack toward the great water.
(The rabbit speaks)
At the end of the point of land
I eat the bark off the tree
I see the track of a lynx
I don't care, I can get away from him
It is a jumping trail
       sep!

WORK STEADILY

Be very careful
    to work steadily
I am afraid they will take you away from me.

I HAVE FOUND MY LOVER

    Oh
        I am thinking
    Oh
        I am thinking
        I have found
        my lover
    Oh
        I think it is so.

MIDÉ SONGS

THESE REPRESENT THE EXPRESSION
OF RELIGIOUS IDEAS

I

   Is it that
      which my voice resembles?

Even metal
      the sounding of my voice?

II

From beneath the high hill
      my voice echoes forth.

III

The strength of metal
      has entered into my arrow point.
A spirit
      I could kill.
The strength of iron
      has entered into my arrow point.

IV

Beautiful as a star hanging in the sky
      is our Midé lodge.

V

I have gained such spirit-power
      that I can tame it in my hand
It is true
      even our white shell
      I can tame it in my hand.

VI

Do not speak ill of the Midé
      my Midé brethren.
Wherever you may be
      do not speak ill of a woman
      my Midé brethren.

VII

We may live by it always
      my Midé brethren
It is spiritual
      the inspiration we receive.

VIII

In the middle of the sea
      in the lengthy room of the sea
      there I am standing.

IX

I that hasten around
I shoot at a man and he falls in a trance
Then I feel with my hand
      to see if he is still alive.

X

My Midé brother
      is searched
In his heart is found
      that which I seek to remove
      a white shell.

XI

Into thy body
      I shoot
      the spirit

XII

What is this
      I promise you?
The skies shall be bright and clear for you
This is what I promise you.

MEMORIAL ODE

Chief John Buck, hereditary Keeper of the Wampum, made and
sung his ode in 1884 on the occasion of the removal of the bones
of Chief Red Jacket from their original burying place to Forest

Lawn Cemetery. The Great League is the League of the five
Iroquois nations in Western New York.

CHANT

Now, listen, Ye who established the Great
      League,
Now it has become old,
Now there is nothing but wilderness.

Ye are in your graves who established it.
Ye have taken it with you and have placed it under you,
And there is nothing left but desert.
There you have taken your great minds.
That which you established, you have taken with you
Ye have placed under your heads what ye have established,
The Great League.

REFRAIN

Woe, Woe! Hearken ye!
      We are diminished
Woe, woe!
      The land has become a thicket.
Woe, woe!
      The clear places are deserted
      They are in their graves who established it.
Woe, the Great League!
      Yet they declared it should endure.
The Great League, Woe!
      Their work has grown old
      We are become wretched. Woe!

SONGS FROM

THE SOUTHEAST

FRAGMENT FROM THE
WALLUM-OLUM OR CHRONICLE
OF THE LENI-LENÂPÉ*

DELAWARE

After the rushing waters had subsided
The Lenâpé of the Turtle were close together,
In hollow houses, living together there.
It freezes where they abode:
It snows where they abode:
It storms where they abode:
It is cold where they abode.
At this northern place they speak favorably
Of mild, cool lands
With many deer and buffaloes.
As they journeyed, some being strong,
Some being rich, they separated
Into house-builders and hunters:
The hunters showed themselves at the north:
The hunters showed themselves at the east:
The hunters showed themselves at the south:
The hunters showed themselves at the west.
In that ancient country, in that northern country,
In that Turtle country
The best of Lenâpé were the Turtle-men.
All the cabin fires of that land were disquieted
And all said, "Let us go."

---

*This famous fragment, the only written (pictograph) historical record
extant among the Eastern tribes, is included as an example of the Saga
element in Indian literature.

To the Snake land, to the east, they went
Going away, earnestly grieving.
Split asunder, weak, trembling, their land burned
They went, torn and broken, to Snake Island.
Those from the north being free, without care
Went forth from the land of snow in different directions.
The fathers of the Bald Eagle and the White Wolf remain
Along the sea, rich in fish and strength.
Floating up stream in their canoes
Our fathers were rich, they were in the light
When they were at those islands.
Head Beaver and Big Bird said:
"Let us go to Snake Island," they said.
All say they will go along
To destroy all the land.
Those of the north agreed,
Those of the east agreed,
Over the sea, the frozen sea,
They went to enjoy it.
On the wonderful slippery water,
On the stone-hard water all went,
On the great tidal sea, the muscle-bearing sea.
Ten thousand at night,
All in one night,
To the Snake Island, to the east, at night,
They walk and walk, all of them.
The men from the north, the east, the south:
The Eagle clan, the Beaver clan, the Wolf clan,
The best men, the rich men, the head men,
Those with wives, those with daughters, those with dogs.
They all come, they tarry at the land of the spruce-pines:
Those from the west come without hesitation,
Esteeming highly their old home at the Turtle land.
There was no rain and no corn
So they moved further seaward.
At the place of caves, in the Buffalo land,
They at last had food on a pleasant plain.

SACRED FORMULAS OF THE CHEROKEES

I

CONCERNING LIVING HUMANITY

LOVE CHARM

Hû! Listen! In Alahí yi you repose, O Terrible Woman,
O you have drawn near to hearken.
There in Elahiyi you are at rest, a White Woman.*
No one is ever lonely when with you.
You are most beautiful.
Instantly and at once you have rendered me a white man.
No one is ever lonely when with me.
Now you have made the path white for me.
It shall never be dreary.
Now you have put me into it.
It shall never become blue.
You have brought down to me from above the white road.
There in mid-earth you have placed me.
I shall stand erect upon the earth.
No one is ever lonely when with me.
I am very handsome.
You have put me into the white house.
I shall be in it as it moves about and no one with me shall
    ever be lonely.
Verily, I shall never become blue.
Instantly you have caused it to be so with me.

And now there in Elahiyi you have rendered the woman blue.
Now you have made the path blue for her.
Let her be completely veiled in loneliness.
Put her into the blue road.
And now bring her down.

---

*White—happy; blue—despondent. "To make lonely" or to be "lonely"
was, to the Cherokees, the depth of degradation.

Place her standing upon the earth.
Where her feet are now and wherever she may go, let
    loneliness leave its mark upon her.
Let her be marked out for loneliness where she stands.

Ha! I belong to the Wolf clan, that one alone which was
    allotted into for you.
No one is ever lonely with me.
I am handsome.
Let her put her soul in the very center of my soul, never to
    turn away.
Grant that, in the midst of men she shall never think of them.
I belong to the one clan alone which was allotted for you
    when the seven clans were established.

Where other men live it is lonely.
They are very loathsome.
The common polecat has made them so like himself that they
    are fit only for his company.
They have become mere refuse.
They are very loathsome.
The common opossum has made them so like himself that
    they are fit only to be with him.
They are very loathsome.
Even the crow has made them so like himself that they are fit
    only for his company.
They are very loathsome.
The miserable rain-crow has made them so like himself that
    they are fit only for his company.

The seven clans all alike make one feel very lonely in their
    company.
They are not even good looking.
They go about clothed with mere refuse.
They even go about covered with dung.
But I—I was ordained to be a white man.

I stand with my face toward the Sun Land.
No one is ever lonely with me.
I am very handsome.
I shall certainly never become blue.
I am covered by the everlasting white house wherever I go.
No one is ever lonely with me.
Your soul has come into the center of my soul, never to turn
    away.
I, Gatigwan asti—I take your soul.
Sge!

II

TO INSURE CONSTANCY

Listen! O, now you have drawn near to harken, O, Ancient
    One.
This woman's soul has come to rest at the edge of your body.
You are never to let go your hold upon it.
It is ordained that you shall do just as you are requested to do.
Let her never think upon any other place.
Her soul has faded within her.
She is bound by the black threads.

III

Listen! "Ha! Now the souls have met, never to part," you
    have said, O Ancient One above.
O Black Spider, you have brought down from on high.
You have let down your web.
She is of the Deer clan; her name is Ayâsta.
Her soul you have wrapped up in your web.

Listen! Ha! But now you have covered her with loneliness.
Her eyes have faded.
Whither can her soul escape?
Let her be sorrowing as she goes along, and not for one night
    alone.

Let her become an aimless wanderer, whose trail may never
be followed.
O Black Spider, may you hold her soul in your web so that it
shall never get through the meshes.
What is the name of the soul?
They two have come together.
It is mine!

Listen! Ha! And now you have harkened,
O Ancient Red.
Your grandchildren have come to the edge of your body.
You hold them yet more firmly in your grasp, never to let go
your hold.
O Ancient One, we have become as one.
The woman has put her soul into our hands.
We shall never let it go!
Yu!

IV

TO DESTROY LIFE

Listen! Now I have come to step over your soul
You are of the Wolf clan.
Your name is A'yû'nini.
Your spittle I have put at rest under the earth.
I have come to cover you over with the black rock.
I have come to cover you over with the black cloth.
I have come to cover you over with the black slabs, never to
reappear.
Toward the black coffin of the upland in the Darkening Land
your paths shall stretch out.
So shall it be for you.
The clay of the upland has come to cover you.
Instantly the black clay has lodged there where it is at rest at
the black houses in the Darkening Land.
With the black coffin and with the black slabs I have come to
cover you.

Now your soul has faded away.
It has become blue.
When darkness comes your spirit shall grow less and dwindle
    away, never to reappear.
Listen!

V

THOSE ABOUT TO BE SLAIN

Ha yi! Yû! Listen!
Now instantly we have lifted up the red war club.
Quickly his soul shall be without motion.
There under the earth, where the black war clubs shall be
    moving about like ball sticks in the game, there his soul
    shall be, never to reappear.
We cause it to be so.
He shall never go and lift up the war club.
We cause it to be so.
There under the earth the black war club and the black fog
    have come together as one for their covering.
The black fog shall never be lifted from them.
We cause it to be so.

SONGS FROM THE

GREAT PLAINS

HUNTING SONGS
DAKOTA

I

Something I've killed, and I lift up my voice;
Something I've killed, and I lift up my voice;
The northern buffalo I've killed, and I lift up my voice;
Something I've killed, and I lift up my voice.

II

The saddle bind:
Children dear.
For half a day,
I will kill.

THE FASHIONING OF THE CHILDREN
OSAGE

CHANT OF THE RED EAGLE CLAN

The First of the Race
Was saying, "Ho, younger brother! the children have no
　　bodies.
"We shall seek bodies for our children.
"Ho, younger brother! you shall attend to it."
They reached one upper world and stood.
There they were not human beings.

"Ho, younger brother! the children have no bodies," he was
    saying.
"We must seek bodies for our children."
They reached the second upper world and stood.
There they were not human beings.
"Ho, younger brother! the children have no bodies," he was
    saying.
"We must seek bodies for our children."
They reached the third upper world and stood.
There they were not human beings.
"Ho, younger brother! the children have no bodies," he was
    saying.
"We must seek bodies for our children."
They reached the fourth upper world and stood.
There they became human beings.
Still, the children were without (human) bodies.
"We must continue to seek bodies for our children."
They returned to the third upper world and stood.
The children were really without bodies.
"Ho, younger brother! the children have no bodies," he was
    saying.
"We must continue to seek bodies for our children."
They returned to the second upper world and stood.
The children did not find bodies for themselves.
"Ho, younger brother! the children have no bodies," he was
    saying.
"We must make an examination awhile longer."
They returned to the first upper world and stood.
They came to red oak and were standing on it.
On a very fine day they came hither and stood.
Kaxe-wahü-sa (the Black Bear), who was then moving,
Came directly to them and stood.
"Ho, elder brother!" (said the Black Bear.)
"You shall continue to burn my feet for me."
"Ho, Kaxe-wahü-sa!" was he (the Tsicu) saying.
Kaxe-wahü-sa went to the star Watse-tuka.
"Ho, grandfather!" he was saying.

"The children have no bodies."

Watse-tuka replied, "Can I give the children bodies?

"I have an everlasting road in which I must keep.

"I am not the only mysterious one;

"You shall attend to it awhile longer."

Then Kaxe-wahü-sa went to the star Watse-mika.

"Ho, grandmother!" he said;

"The children have no bodies."

She replied, "Can I give bodies to the children?

"I have an everlasting road in which I must keep.

"I am not the only mysterious one!

"You shall attend to it awhile longer."

Then he went to the mysterious one of day.

"Ho, grandfather!" said he;

"The children have no bodies."

Said he, "Can I give the children bodies?

"I have an everlasting road in which I must keep.

"I am not the only mysterious one;

"You shall attend to it awhile longer."

Then he went to the mysterious one of night.

"Ho, grandfather!" said he;

"The children have no bodies, grandfather!"

The Moon replied, "Can I give bodies to the children?

"I have an everlasting road in which I must keep.

"I am not the only mysterious one;

"You shall attend to it awhile longer."

Then he went to the Pleiades, saying,

"Ho, grandfathers!

"The children have no bodies."

One of these replied, "Can I give bodies to the children!

"I have an everlasting road in which I must keep.

"I am not the only mysterious one;

"You shall attend to it awhile longer."

Then he went to the constellation called Three Deer.

"Ho, grandfather," said he;

"The children have no bodies."

The latter replied, "Can I give the children bodies?

"I have an everlasting road in which I must keep.

"I am not the only mysterious one;

"You shall attend to it awhile longer."

Then he went to the Morning Star, saying,

"Ho, grandfather!

"The children have no bodies."

The star replied, "Can I give bodies to the children?

"I have an everlasting road in which I must keep.

"I am not the only mysterious one;

"You shall attend to it awhile longer."

Then he went to the Small Star, saying,

"Ho, grandfather!

"The children have no bodies."

The star replied, "Can I give bodies to the children?

"I have an everlasting road in which I must keep.

"I am not the only mysterious one;

"You shall attend to it awhile longer."

The female Red Bird, who had been moving, was sitting on
     her nest.

To her he came, saying,

"Ho, grandmother!

"The children have no bodies."

She replied, "I can cause your children to have (human)
     bodies from my own.

"My left wing shall be a left arm for the children.

"My right wing shall be a right arm for them.

"My head shall be a head for them.

"My mouth shall be a mouth for them.

"My forehead shall be a forehead for them.

"My neck shall be a neck for them.

"My throat shall be a throat for them.

"My chest shall be a chest for them.

"My thighs shall be thighs for them.

"My knees shall be knees for them.

"My heels shall be their heels.

"My toes shall be their toes.

"My claws shall be their toenails.

"You shall live forever without destruction.
"Your children shall live as human beings.
"The speech of children I will bestow on your children."

THE CHILD IS INTRODUCED TO THE COSMOS AT BIRTH
OMAHA

Ho! Ye Sun, Moon, Stars, all ye that move in the heavens,
      I bid you hear me!
Into your midst has come a new life.
      Consent ye, I implore!
Make its path smooth, that it may reach the brow of the first
  hill!

Ho! Ye Winds, Clouds, Rain, Mist, all ye that move in the
  air,
      I bid you hear me!
Into your midst has come a new life.
      Consent ye, I implore!
Make its path smooth, that it may reach the brow of the
  second hill!
Ho! Ye Hills, Valleys, Rivers, Lakes, Trees, Grasses, all ye of
  the earth,
      I bid you hear me!
Into your midst has come a new life.
      Consent ye, I implore!
Make its path smooth, that it may reach the brow of the
  third hill!
Ho! Ye Birds, great and small, that fly in the air,
Ho! Ye Animals, great and small, that dwell in the forest,
Ho! Ye insects that creep among the grasses and burrow in
  the ground—
      I bid you hear me!
Into your midst has come a new life.
      Consent ye, I implore!

Make its path smooth, that it may reach the brow of the
   fourth hill!

Ho! All ye of the heavens, all ye of the air, all ye of the
   earth:
        I bid you all to hear me!
Into your midst has come a new life.
            Consent ye, consent ye all, I implore!
Make its path smooth—then shall it travel beyond the four
   hills!

RITUAL CHANT AT THE PREPARATION OF
THE SWEAT LODGE FOR THE SICK
OMAHA

*The Stone, with the curative powers of its heat, becomes a symbol
of permanency and strength.*
Ho! Aged One, eçka,*
At a time when there were gathered together seven persons,
You sat in the seventh place, it is said,
And of the Seven you alone possessed knowledge of all things,
        Aged One, eçka.
When in their longing for protection and guidance,
The people sought in their minds for a way,
They beheld you sitting with assured permanency and
   endurance
In the center where converged the paths,
There, exposed to the violence of the four winds, you sat,
Possessed with power to receive supplications,
        Aged One, eçka.
Where is his mouth, by which there may be utterance of
   speech?
Where is his heart, to which there may come knowledge and
   understanding?

---

*Eçka—I implore.

Where are his feet, whereby he may move from place to
    place?
We question in wonder,
Yet verily it is said you alone have power to receive
    supplications,
            Aged One, eçka.
I have desired to go yet farther in the path of life with my
    little ones,
Without pain, without sickness,
Beyond the second, third, and fourth period of life's pathway,
            Aged One, eçka.
O hear! This is my prayer,
Although uttered in words poorly put together,
            Aged One, eçka.

RITUAL CHANT FOR THE SICK
OMAHA

He! Aged One, eçka
Thou Rock, eçka
Aged One, eçka
He! I have taught these little ones
They obey, eçka
Aged One, eçka
He!
He! Unmoved from time without end, verily
Thou sittest, eçka
In the midst of the various paths of the coming winds
In the midst of the winds thou sittest, eçka
Aged One, eçka
He! The small grasses grow about thee, eçka
Thou sittest as though making of them thy dwelling place,
    eçka
He! Verily thou sittest covered with the droppings of birds,
    eçka
Thy head decked with the downy feathers of the birds, eçka

Aged One, eçka
Thou who standest next in power, eçka
He! thou water, eçka
Water that hast been flowing
From time unknown, eçka
He! Of you the little ones have taken
Though thy mysteries remain unrevealed
These little ones crave thy touch, eçka
He! Thou that standest as one dwelling place, eçka
Even as one dwelling place, eçka
Ye great animals, eçka
He! Who make for us the covering, eçka
These little ones, thou hast said, let their thoughts reverently
    dwell on me, eçka
He! Thou tent frame, eçka
Thou standest with bent back o'er us
With stooping shoulders, bending over us
Verily, thou standest
Thus my little ones shall speak of me, thou hast said
Brushing back the hair from thy forehead, eçka
The hair of thy head
The grass that grows about thee
Thy hairs are whitened, eçka
The hairs that grow upon thy head, eçka
O, the paths that the little ones shall take, eçka
Whichever way they may flee from danger, eçka
They shall escape. Their shoulders shall be bent with age as
    they walk
As they walk on the well-beaten path
Shading their brows now and again with their hands
As they walk in their old age, eçka
That of thy strength they shall partake, eçka
Therefore thy little ones desire to walk closely by thy side,
    eçka
Venerable One, eçka.

RITUAL OF THE COSMIC FORCES
OMAHA

Toward the coming of the sun
There the people of every kind gathered,
And great animals of every kind.
Verily all gathered together, as well as people.
Insects also of every description,
Verily all gathered there together,
By what means or manner we know not.
Verily, one alone of all these was the greatest,
Inspiring to all minds,
The great white rock,
Standing and reaching as high as the heavens, enwrapped in
    mist,
Verily as high as the heavens.
Thus my little ones shall speak of me,
As long as they shall travel in life's path, thus they shall speak
    of me.
Such was the words, it has been said.
Then next in rank
Thou, male of the crane, stoodst with thy long beak
And thy neck, none like to it in length,
There with thy beak didst thou strike the earth.

———

This shall be the legend
Of the people of yore, the red people,
Thus my little ones shall speak of me.
Then next in rank stood the male gray wolf, whose cry,
Though uttered without effort, verily made the earth to
    tremble,
Even the stable earth to tremble.
Such shall be the legend of the people.
Then next in rank stood Hega, the buzzard, with his red neck.
Calmly he stood, his great wings spread, letting the heat of the
    sun straighten his feathers.
Slowly he flapped his wings,

Then floated away, as though without effort,
Thus displaying a power (a gift of Wakonda) often to be
   spoken of by the old men in their teachings.

SONG OF SCORN
OMAHA

Ena! The one I wish to marry has gone to war.
Ena! The one I hate has not gone forth but remains here.

THE GHOST-DANCE RELIGION

In 1892 the last serious Indian outbreak occurred. This was oc-
casioned by the government's efforts to suppress the practices
of a new religion which, during the two years preceding, had
spread over a large part of the west, among the Indian tribes
from the Plains to the Coast, and from the Columbia to the
Rio Grande. The Prophet of this new cult claimed to be the
Messiah, and professed to exercise divine powers. He instituted
certain dances, which his followers, in a vain attempt to over-
throw the world-order magically, perverted into frenzied
rites, wherein entranced, they saw visions and spoke with the
dead. The Messiah concept is an ancient one in Indian mythol-
ogy, antedating all Christian influence, and so desperate had be-
come the straits of the Vanishing Race that these doctrines
received wide acceptance. At length the government intervened
and brought the strange worship to an end.

Mr. James Mooney investigated this interesting phenome-
non and actually discovered the Seer, who proved to be an in-
offensive visionary dwelling in a remote valley of the Southwest.
This young man's life and theories (a full-blood, apparently un-
touched by Christian influence), curiously resembled those of
Christ, and like the latter, he preached the doctrines of Non-
resistance and the Brotherhood of Man. In this case our govern-
ment played the part of Rome.

These songs were sung during the dancing, and express in the image of the Whirlwind, a mystic and exalted contemplation of the approaching Great Change. Unessential repetitions have been omitted for brevity's sake.

SONGS OF THE GHOST-DANCE RELIGION
ARAPAHO

DISILLUSION

I

My children, when at first I liked the Whites,
My children, when at first I liked the Whites,
I gave them fruits,
I gave them fruits.

ECSTASY

II

My children, my children,
The wind makes the head-feathers sing—
The wind makes the head-feathers sing.
My children, my children.

LABORS OF THE SPIRIT

III

My children, my children,
I take pity on those who have been taught,
Because they push on hard,
Says our Father.

WONDER

IV

How bright is the moonlight!
Tonight as I ride with my load of buffalo beef.

THE WHIRLWIND (POWER OF CHANGE) SPEAKS

V

I circle around
The boundaries of earth,
Wearing the long wing feathers as I fly.

VISION

VI

My children, my children,
Look! the earth is about to move.
My Father tells me so.

SPIRIT-JOY

VII

I fly around yellow,
I fly with the wild rose on my head,
On high—He'e'e'!

REVELATION

VIII

My children, my children,
It is I who wear the morning star on my head;
I show it to my children,
Says the Father.

TRAVAIL OF SPIRIT

IX

Father, have pity on me,
Father, have pity on me;
I am crying for thirst;
All is gone—I have nothing to eat.

INVOCATION

X

Father, the Morning Star!
Father, the Morning Star!
Look on us, we have danced until daylight,
Take pity on us—Hi'i'i!

THE MESSIAH SPEAKS
CHEYENNE

I am coming in sight—
I bring the Whirlwind with me—
That you may know one another.

REINCARNATION
COMANCHE

We shall live again,
We shall live again.
The sun's beams are spreading out—He'e'yo'!
The sun's yellow rays are spreading out—Ahi'ni'yo'!

SONGS OF LIFE RETURNING
PAIUTE

I

The wind stirs the willows.
The wind stirs the grasses.

II

The cottonwoods are growing tall,
They are growing tall and verdant.

III

A slender antelope,
A slender antelope
He is wallowing upon the ground.

IV

Fog! Fog!
Lightning! Lightning!
Whirlwind! Whirlwind!

V

Whirlwind! Whirlwind!
The snowy earth comes gliding, the snowy earth comes
gliding.

VI

There is dust from the whirlwind,
There is dust from the whirlwind,
The whirlwind on the mountain.

VII

The rocks are ringing.
The rocks are ringing,
They are ringing in the mountains.

SONG OF THE PATH OF SOULS

VIII

The snow lies there—ro'rani!
The snow lies there—ro'rani!
The milky way lies there!

CREATION
SIOUX

I

This is my work—Yo'yoyo'!
All that grows upon the earth is mine—Yo'yoyo'!
Says the Father—Yo'yoyo'!
E'ya Yo'yoyo'!

LAMENT

II

Mother, come home; mother, come home.
My little brother goes about always crying,
My little brother goes about always crying.
Mother, come home; mother come home.

COURIER CHANT

III

He! They have come back racing,
Why, they say there is to be a buffalo hunt over here,
Why, they say there is to be a buffalo hunt over here,
Make arrows! Make arrows!
Says the Father, says the Father.

THE MILLENIUM

IV

The whole world is coming,
A nation is coming, a nation is coming,
The Eagle has brought the message to the tribe.
Over the whole earth they are coming;
The buffalo are coming, the buffalo are coming,
The Crow has brought the message to the tribe.

JUDGMENT

KIOWA

I

The Father will descend.
Everybody will arise.
Stretch out your hands.
The earth will tremble.

VISITATION

II

The spirit army is approaching,
The whole world is moving onward.
See! Everybody is standing watching.
Let us all pray.

THE SECRET OF HUMANITY

III

Because I am poor,
I pray for every living creature.

THE GOD-MAN

IV

My Father has had pity on me.
I have eyes like my Father's,
I have hands like my Father's,
I have legs like my Father's,
I have a form like my Father's.

THE SPIRIT HUNTERS

V

The spirit host is advancing, they say.
They are coming with the buffalo, they say.
They are coming with the new earth, they say.

MYSTIC

VI

That wind, that wind
Shakes my tipi, shakes my tipi,
And sings a song for me,
And sings a song for me.

EXHORTATION
CADDO

Come on, Caddo, we are all going up,
Come on, Caddo, we are all going up
To the great village—He'e'ye'!
To the great village—He'e'ye'!
With our Father above,
With our Father above when he dwells on high—He'e'ye!
Where our Mother dwells—Hhe'e'ye'!
Where our Mother dwells—Hhe'e'ye'!

SONGS FROM
THE SOUTHWEST

VIRACOCHA

ANCIENT INCA

Beautiful Princess
Lo, thy brother
Breaks thy vessel
Now in fragments.
From the blow comes
Thunder, lightning,
Strokes of lightning.
And thou, princess,
Take the water;
As the rain, fall;
As the hail, fall;
As the snow, fall;
Viracocha
World-dispenser.

WAR SONGS

ZUÑI

To you of the six regions
Whose homes cover the earth
I give shells.
Yellow ant, blue ant, red ant, all color ant
U—hu—we—u—hu—we—
U—hu—we—u—hu—we.
To you whose homes
Are covered with mountain tops

I give shells
Yellow, blue, red, white, all color, black.
When we meet the enemy
A little arrow storm will arise.
When we meet him on the road nearby
He will never more inhale the sacred breath of day.
I inhale the sacred breath of day.
All come quickly,
The enemy comes from ambush.
A Navajo is killed,
We inhale the sacred breath of day.

You have met the enemy.
He will never more inhale the sacred breath of day.
The enemy is destroyed.
Who will be our great Bow priest?
Who is to become a Bow priest?
Well! who will kick the scalp?
His younger mother, his elder sister.
Who will wash the scalp?
His younger father, his elder brother.
Well!
Good!

PRAYER FOR RAIN

SIA

White floating clouds,
Clouds like the plains
Come and water the earth.
Sun embrace the earth
That she may be fruitful.
Moon, lion of the north,
Bear of the west,
Badger of the south,
Wolf of the east,

Eagle of the heavens,
Shrew of the earth,
Elder war hero,
Warriors of the six mountains of the world,
Intercede with the cloud people for us,
That they may water the earth.
Medicine bowl, cloud bowl, and water vase
Give us your hearts,
That the earth may be watered.
I make the ancient road of meal,
That my song may pass over it—
The ancient road.
White shell bead woman
Who lives where the sun goes down,
Mother Whirlwind,
Father Sus'sistinnako,
Mother Ya'ya, creator of good thoughts.
Yellow woman of the north,
Blue woman of the west,
Red woman of the south,
White woman of the east,
Slightly yellow woman of the zenith,
And dark woman of the nadir,
I ask your intercession with the cloud people.

RAIN SONG OF THE GIANT SOCIETY

S I A

We, the Ancient Ones,
Who ascended from the middle of the world below,
Our medicine is precious,
It is as our hearts precious to us,
Arrow of lightning
Come to us
Echo.
Spruce of the north

And all your people;
Your thoughts come to us.
Who is it?
White floating clouds.
May your thoughts come to us
And all your people,
May their thoughts come to us.
Who is it?
Clouds like the plains,
May your thoughts come to us.
Who is it?
Arrow of lightning,
May your thoughts come to us.
Who is it?
Earth horizon
And all your people,
May your thoughts come to us.

INVOCATION TO THE U'WANNAMI
SIA

I

Come you, ascend the ladder; all come in; all sit down.
We were poor, poor, poor, poor, poor, poor,
When we came to this world through the poor place,
Where the body of water dried for our passing.
Banked up clouds cover the earth.
All come four times with your showers,
Descend to the base of the ladder and stand still;
Bring your showers and great rains.
All, all come, all ascend, all come in, all sit down.

II

I throw out to you my sacred meal that you may all come.
Hold your gaming-stick; throw it forward; all come.

All come out and give us your showers and great rains; all
    come,
That the seeds may be strong and come up, that all seed plants
    may come up and be strong.
Come you that all trees and seeds may come up and be strong.
Come you hither; all come.

III

Cover my earth mother four times with many flowers.
Let the heavens be covered with the banked up clouds.
Let the earth be covered with fog; cover the earth with rains.
Great waters, rains, cover the earth. Lightning cover the earth.
Let thunder be heard over the earth; let thunder be heard;
Let thunder be heard over the six regions of the earth.

IV

Rain-makers, come out from all roads that great rivers may
    cover the earth;
That stones may be moved by the torrents;
That trees may be uprooted and moved by the torrents.
Great rain-makers, come out from all roads, carry the sands of
    our earth mother of the place.
Cover the earth with her heart, that all seeds may develop,
That my children may have all things to eat and be happy;
That the people of the outlying villages may all laugh and be
    happy;
That the growing children may all have things to eat and be
    happy.
This way our great father wishes you to come.
This way our great mother wishes you to come.
That we may have all kinds of seeds and all things good;
That we may inhale the sacred breath of life;
That our fathers and our mothers may bring us happy days.
Let our children live and be happy.
Send us the good south winds.
Send us your breath over the lakes that our great world may
    be made beautiful and our people may live.

V

There, far off, my Sun Father arises, ascends the ladder, comes
  forth from his place.
May all complete the road of life, may all grow old.
May the children inhale more of the sacred breath of life.
May all my children have corn that they may complete the
  road of life.
Here sit down; here remain; we give you our best thoughts.
Hasten over the meal road; we are jealous of you.
We inhale the sacred breath through our prayer plumes.

MAGPIE SONG
NAVAJO

The Magpie! The Magpie! Here underneath
In the white of his wings are the footsteps of morning.
It dawns! It dawns!

SONGS IN THE GARDEN OF THE HOUSE GOD
NAVAJO

I

Truly in the East
The white bean
And the great corn-plant
Are tied with the white lightning.
Listen! rain approaches!
The voice of the bluebird is heard.
Truly in the East
The white bean
And the great squash
Are tied with the rainbow,

Listen! rain approaches!
The voice of the bluebird is heard.

II

From the top of the great corn-plant the water gurgles, I hear
it;
Around the roots the water foams, I hear it;
Around the roots of the plants it foams, I hear it;
From their tops the water foams, I hear it.

III

The corn grows up. The waters of the dark clouds drop, drop.
The rain descends. The waters from the corn leaves drop,
drop.
The rain descends. The waters from the plants drop, drop.
The corn grows up. The waters of the dark mists drop, drop.

IV

Shall I cull this fruit of the great corn-plant?
Shall you break it? Shall I break it?
Shall I break it? Shall you break it?
Shall I? Shall you?
Shall I cull this fruit of the great squash vine?
Shall you pick it up? Shall I pick it up?
Shall I pick it up? Shall you pick it up?
Shall I? Shall you?

THE MOUNTAIN CHANT OF THE NAVAJO

CHARACTER OF THE SONGS

Some songs are self-explanatory or readily understood, but the
greater number cannot be comprehended without a full knowl-
edge of the mythology and of the symbolism to which they
refer; they merely hint at mythic conceptions. Many contain
archaic expressions, for which the shaman can assign a meaning,

but whose etymology cannot now be learned; and some embody obsolete words whose meaning is lost even to the priesthood. There are many vocables known to be meaningless and recited merely to fill out the rhythm or to give a dignified length to the song. For the same reasons a meaningless syllable is often added or a significant syllable duplicated.

Other poetical licenses are taken, such as the omission of a syllable, the change of accent, the substitution of one vowel for another. The most familiar words are often distorted beyond recognition. For these various reasons the task of noting and translating these songs is one of considerable difficulty. In order to simplify the meaning of certain chants repetitive phrases are set as refrains.

PRELUDE

INVOCATION TO DSILYI N'EYANI

Reared Within the Mountains!
Lord of the Mountains!
Young Man!
Chieftain!
I have made your sacrifice.
I have prepared a smoke for you.
My feet restore thou for me.
My legs restore thou for me.
My body restore thou for me.
My mind restore thou for me.
My voice restore thou for me.
Restore all for me in beauty.
Make beautiful all that is before me.
Make beautiful all that is behind me.
It is done in beauty.
It is done in beauty.
It is done in beauty.
It is done in beauty.

FIRST SONG OF THE THUNDER

Thonah! Thonah!
There is a voice above,
The voice of the thunder.
Within the dark cloud,
Again and again it sounds,
Thonah! Thonah!
Thonah! Thonah!
There is a voice below,
The voice of the grasshopper.
Among the plants,
Again and again it sounds,
Thonah! Thonah!

II

TWELFTH SONG OF THE THUNDER

The voice that beautifies the land!
The voice above,
The voice of the thunder
Within the dark cloud
Again and again it sounds,
The voice that beautifies the land!
The voice that beautifies the land!
The voice below;
The voice of the grasshopper
Among the plants
Again and again it sounds,
The voice that beautifies the land!

III

FIRST SONG OF THE EXPLODING STICK

Young Woman Who Becomes a Bear set fire in the mountains

In many places; as she journeyed on
There was a line of burning mountains.
The Otter set fire in the waters
In many places; as he journeyed on
There was a line of burning waters.

IV

LAST SONG OF THE EXPLODING STICK

Maid Who Becomes a Bear sought the gods and found them;
On the high mountain peaks she sought the gods and found
   them;
Truly with my sacrifice she sought the gods and found them.
Somebody doubts it, so I have heard.

V

FIRST DAYLIGHT SONG

The curtain of daybreak is hanging,
The Daylight Boy (it is hanging),
From the land of day it is hanging;
Before him, as it dawns, it is hanging;
Behind him, as it dawns, it is hanging.
Before him, in beauty, it is hanging;
Behind him, in beauty, it is hanging;
From his voice, in beauty, it is hanging.

VI

LAST DAYLIGHT SONG

Lullaby, lullaby.
It is daybreak. Lullaby.
Now comes the Daylight Boy. Lullaby.

Now it is day. Lullaby.
Now comes the Daylight Girl. Lullaby.

VII

SONG OF THE PROPHET

That flowing water! That flowing water!
My mind wanders across it.
That broad water! That flowing water!
My mind wanders across it.
That old age water! That flowing water!
My mind wanders across it.

VIII

SONG OF THE RISING SUN DANCE

Where the sun rises,
The Holy Young Man
The great plumed arrow
Has swallowed
And withdrawn it.
The sun
Is satisfied.
Where the sun sets,
The Holy Young Woman
The cliff rose arrow
Has swallowed
And withdrawn it.
The moon
Is satisfied.

IX

LAST WORDS OF THE PROPHET

Farewell, my younger brother!
From the holy places the gods come for me.
You will never see me again; but when the showers pass and
    the thunders peal,
"There," you will say, "is the voice of my elder brother."
And when the harvest comes, of the beautiful birds and
    grasshoppers you will say,
"There is the ordering of my elder brother!"

SONG OF BÉKOTSIDI WHEN HE
MADE THINGS

*Both of the gods sang while they were at work, and this was the
song that Békotsidi sang to bless all that he was making. It was the
first song which he sang at this work.*

Now Békotsidi, that am I.
    For them I make.
Now child of Day Bearer am I.
    For them I make.
Now Day Bearer's beam of blue.
    For them I make.
Shines on my feet and your feet too.
    For them I make.
Horses of all kinds now increase.
    For them I make.
At my fingers' tips and yours.
    For them I make.
Beasts of all kinds now increase.
    For them I make.
The bluebirds now increase.
    For them I make.
Soft goods of all kinds now increase.

For them I make.
Now with the pollen they increase.
For them I make.
Increasing now, they will last forever.
For them I make.
In old age wandering on the trail of beauty.
For them I make.
To form them fair, for them I labor.
For them I make.

SONGS OF DAWN BOY

I

Where my kindred dwell,
There I wander.
The Red Rock House,
There I wander.
Where dark kethawns are at the doorway,
There I wander.
With the pollen of dawn upon my trail,
There I wander.
At the yuni, the striped cotton hangs with pollen.
There I wander.
Going around with it.
There I wander.
Taking another, I depart with it.
With it I wander.
In the house of long life,
There I wander.
In the house of happiness,
There I wander.
Beauty before me,
With it I wander.
Beauty behind me,
With it I wander.

Beauty below me,
> *With it I wander.*

Beauty above me,
> *With it I wander.*

Beauty all around me,
> *With it I wander.*

In old age traveling,
> *With it I wander.*

On the beautiful trail I am,
> *With it I wander.*

II

In Kininaéki.
In the house made of dawn.
In the story made of dawn.
On the trail of dawn.
O, Talking God!
His feet, my feet, restore
His limbs, my limbs, restore.
His body, my body, restore.
His mind, my mind, restore.
His voice, my voice, restore.
His plumes, my plumes, restore.
With beauty before him, with beauty before me.
With beauty behind him, with beauty behind me.
With beauty above him, with beauty below me.
With beauty below him, with beauty below me.
With beauty around him, with beauty around me.
With pollen beautiful in his voice, with pollen beautiful in my
    voice.
It is finished in beauty.
It is finished in beauty.
In the house of evening light.
From the story made of evening light.
On the trail of evening light.
O, House God!
(The rest as in I, except that lines 12 and 13 are transposed.)

III

To the house of my kindred,
>   *There I return.*
Child of the yellow corn am I.
To the Red Rock House,
>   *There I return.*
Where the blue kethawns are by the doorway,
>   *There I return.*
The pollen of evening light on my trail,
>   *There I return.*
At the yuni the haliotis shell hangs with the pollen,
Going around,
>   *With it I return.*
Taking another, I walk out with it.
>   *With it I return.*
To the house of old age,
>   *Up there I return.*
To the house of happiness,
>   *Up there I return.*
Beauty behind me,
>   *With it I return.*
Beauty before me,
>   *With it I return.*
Beauty above me,
>   *With it I return.*
Beauty below me,
>   *With it I return.*
Beauty all around me,
>   *With it I return.*
Now in old age wandering,
>   *I return.*
Now on the trail of beauty, I am.
>   *There I return.*

A PRAYER

FOR SECOND DAY OF THE NIGHT CHANT

From the base of the east.
From the base of the Pelado Peak.
From the house made of mirage,
From the story made of mirage,
From the doorway of rainbow,
The path out of which is the rainbow,
The rainbow passed out with me.
The rainbow raised up with me.
Through the middle of broad fields,
The rainbow returned with me.
To where my house is visible,
The rainbow returned with me.
To the roof of my house,
The rainbow returned with me.
To the entrance of my house.
The rainbow returned with me.
To just within my house,
The rainbow returned with me.
To my fireside,
The rainbow returned with me.
To the center of my house,
The rainbow returned with me.
At the fore part of my house with the dawn,
The Talking God sits with me.
The House God sits with me.
Pollen Boy sits with me.
Grasshopper Girl sits with me.
In beauty Estsánatlehi, my mother, for her I return.
Beautifully my fire to me is restored.
Beautifully my possessions are to me restored.
Beautifully my soft goods to me are restored.
Beautifully my hard goods to me are restored.
Beautifully my horses to me are restored.

Beautifully my sheep to me are restored.
Beautifully my old men to me are restored.
Beautifully my old women to me are restored.
Beautifully my young men to me are restored.
Beautifully my women to me are restored.
Beautifully my children to me are restored.
Beautifully my wife to me is restored.
Beautifully my chiefs to me are restored.
Beautifully my country to me is restored.
Beautifully my fields to me are restored.
Beautifully my house to me is restored.
Talking God sits with me.
House God sits with me.
Pollen Boy sits with me.
Grasshopper Girl sits with me.
Beautifully white corn to me is restored.
Beautifully yellow corn to me is restored.
Beautifully blue corn to me is restored.
Beautifully corn of all kinds to me is restored.
In beauty may I walk.
All day long may I walk.
Through the returning seasons may I walk.
On the trail marked with pollen may I walk.
With grasshoppers about my feet may I walk.
With dew about my feet may I walk.
With beauty may I walk.
With beauty before me, may I walk.
With beauty behind me, may I walk.
With beauty above me, may I walk.
With beauty below me, may I walk.
With beauty all around me, may I walk.
In old age wandering on a trail of beauty, lively, may I walk.
In old age wandering on a trail of beauty, living again, may I
    walk.
It is finished in beauty.
It is finished in beauty.

NIGHT CHANT

FOR THE NINTH SONG

In Tsegihi,
In the house made of dawn,
In the house made of evening twilight,
In the house made of dark cloud,
In the house made of rain and mist, of pollen, of grasshoppers,
Where the dark mist curtains the doorway,
The path to which is on the rainbow,
Where the zig-zag lightning stands high on top,
Where the he-rain stands high on top,
Oh, male divinity!
With your moccasins of dark clouds, come to us,
With your mind enveloped in dark cloud, come to us,
With the dark thunder above you, come to us soaring,
With the shapen cloud at your feet, come to us soaring.
With the far darkness made of the dark cloud over your head,
    come to us soaring,
With the far darkness made of the rain and the mist over your
    head, come to us soaring,
With the far darkness made of the rain and the mist over your
    head, come to us soaring.
With the zig-zag lightning flung out high over your head,
With the rainbow hanging high over your head, come to us
    soaring.
With the far darkness made of the dark cloud on the ends of
    your wings,
With the far darkness made of the rain and the mist on the
    ends of your wings, come to us soaring,
With the zig-zag lightning, with the rainbow hanging high on
    the ends of your wings, come to us soaring.
With the near darkness made of dark cloud of the rain and the
    mist, come to us,
With the darkness on the earth, come to us.

———

With these I wish the foam floating on the flowing water
over the roots of the great corn,
I have made your sacrifice,
I have prepared a smoke for you,
My feet restore for me.
My limbs restore, my body restore, my mind restore, my
voice restore for me.
Today, take out your spell for me,
Today, take away your spell for me.
Away from me you have taken it,
Far off from me it is taken,
Far off you have done it.

Happily I recover,
Happily I become cool,
My eyes regain their power, my head cools, my limbs regain
their strength, I hear again.
Happily for me the spell is taken off,
Happily I walk; impervious to pain, I walk; light within, I
walk; joyous, I walk.
Abundant dark clouds I desire,
An abundance of vegetation I desire,
An abundance of pollen, abundant dew, I desire.
Happily may fair white corn, to the ends of the earth, come
with you,
Happily may fair yellow corn, fair blue corn, fair corn of all
kinds, plants of all kinds, goods of all kinds, jewels of all
kinds, to the ends of the earth, come with you.
With these before you, happily may they come with you,
With these behind, below, above, around you, happily may
they come with you,
Thus you accomplish your tasks.

Happily the old men will regard you,
Happily the old women will regard you,
The young men and the young women will regard you,
The children will regard you,

The chiefs will regard you,
Happily, as they scatter in different directions, they will
    regard you,
Happily, as they approach their homes, they will regard you.

May their roads home be on the trail of peace,
Happily may they all return.
In beauty I walk,
With beauty before me, I walk,
With beauty behind me, I walk,
With beauty above and about me, I walk,
It is finished in beauty,
It is finished in beauty.

PROTECTION SONG
NAVAJO

TO BE SUNG ON GOING INTO BATTLE

I

Now, Slayer of the Alien Gods, among men am I.
Now among the alien gods with weapons of magic am I.
Rubbed with the summits of the mountains,
Now among the alien gods with weapons of magic am I.
Now upon the beautiful trail of old age,
Now among the alien gods with weapons of magic am I.

II

Now, Offspring of the Water, among men am I.
Now among the alien gods with weapons of magic am I.
Rubbed with the water of the summits,
Now among the alien gods with weapons of magic am I.
Now upon the beautiful trail of old age,
Now among the alien gods with weapons of magic am I.

III

Now, Lightning of the Thunder, among men am I.
Now among the alien gods with weapons of magic am I.
Rubbed with the summit of the sky,
Now among the alien gods with weapons of magic am I.
Now upon the beautiful trail of old age,
Now among the alien gods with weapons of magic am I.

IV

Now, Altsodoniglehi, among men am I.
Now among the alien gods with weapons of magic am I.
Rubbed with the summits of the earth,
Now among the alien gods with weapons of magic am I.
Now upon the beautiful trail of old age,
Now among the alien gods with weapons of magic am I.

THE TOWN CRIER CALLS AT DAWN TO ANNOUNCE THE FEAST

PUEBLO

All people awake, open your eyes, arise,
Become children of light, vigorous, active, sprightly.
Hasten clouds from the four world quarters;
Come snow in plenty, that water may be abundant when
    summer comes;
Come ice, cover the fields, that the planting may yield
    abundance,
Let all hearts be glad!
The knowing ones will assemble in four days;
They will encircle the village dancing and singing songs . . .
That moisture may come in abundance.

SONG OF THE HORSE
NAVAJO

How joyous his neigh!
Lo, the Turquoise Horse of Johano-ai,
How joyous his neigh,
There on precious hides outspread standeth he;
How joyous his neigh,
There on tips of fair fresh flowers feedeth he;
How joyous his neigh,
There of mingled waters holy drinketh he;
How joyous his neigh,
There he spurneth dust of glittering grains;
How joyous his neigh,
There in mist of sacred pollen hidden, all hidden he;
How joyous his neigh,
There his offspring many grow and thrive for evermore;
How joyous his neigh!

SONG OF THE BLUE-CORN DANCE
ZUÑI

Beautiful, lo, the summer clouds,
Beautiful, lo, the summer clouds!
Blossoming clouds in the sky,
Like unto shimmering flowers,
Blossoming clouds in the sky,
Onward, lo, they come,
Hither, hither bound!

PIMA RITUAL SONG CYCLE
THE FLOOD

I

ELDER BROTHER, SON OF EARTH

(Chanted by the People)
Dazzling power has Elder Brother,
      Mastering the winds with song.
Swiftly now we come together,
      Singing to gain control.

II

EARTH DOCTOR PROPHESIED THE FLOOD, CAUSED BY ELDER BROTHER:

Weep, my unfortunate people!
      All this you will see take place.
Weep, my unfortunate people!
      For the waters will overwhelm the land.
Weep, my unhappy relatives!
      You will learn all.
Weep, my unfortunate relatives!
      You will learn all.
The waters will overwhelm the mountains.

III

ELDER BROTHER FROM HIS OLLA SONG:

Black house! Black house! Hold me safely in;
Black house! Black house! Hold me safely in,
      As I journey to and fro, to and fro.

AS HE WAS BORNE ALONG BY THE FLOOD HE SANG:

Running water, running water, herein resounding,
As on the clouds I am carried to the sky,
Running water, running water, herein roaring,
As on the clouds I am carried to the sky.

EMERGING SAFELY FROM THE OLLA HE SANG:

Here I come forth! Here I come forth!
With magic powers I emerge.
Here I come forth! Here I come forth!
With magic powers I emerge.
I stand alone! Alone!
Who will accompany me?
My staff and my crystal
They shall bide with me.

IV

HOW SOUTH DOCTOR FORETOLD THE DESTRUCTION OF EARTH AND ALL ITS CREATURES:

The waters dissolve the land.
The waters dissolve the land.
The mighty magician tests his strength.
The waters dissolve the mountain.
The waters dissolve the mountain.
Nasi foresees what is coming.

V

EARTH DOCTOR BEHELD THE RISING WATERS:

Haiya! Haiya! Flood! Flood! Hai-iya!
See the doom awaiting them!

Haiya! Haiya! Flood! Flood! Hai-iya!
　　　Here are my doomed people before me.

VI

SOUTH DOCTOR RAISED THE MOUNTAINS:

On the Crooked mountain I am standing,
　　　Trying to disperse the waters.
On the Crooked mountain I am standing,
　　　Trying to disperse the waters.

AND MARKED THE LIMITS OF THE FLOOD:

On the Crooked mountain top I'm standing,
　　　Trying to disperse the waters.
On the Crooked mountain top I'm standing,
　　　Trying to disperse the waters.

BUT HE COULD DO NO MORE:

Powerless! Powerless!
　　　Powerless is my magic crystal!
Powerless! Powerless!
　　　I shall become as stone.

*Earth Doctor escaped destruction by shutting himself in his reed
　　staff.*
Elder Brother was saved in his olla.
　　After the waters rolled back
*Elder Brother was first to appear and so became ruler of the
　　world.*
Now Earth Doctor created all things anew.

CREATION SONGS BY EARTH DOCTOR

I

Earth Magician shapes this world.
Behold what he can do!
Round and smooth he molds it.
Behold what he can do!

II

Earth Magician makes the mountains.
Heed what he has to say!
He it is that makes the mesas.
Heed what he has to say.
Earth Magician shapes this world;
Earth Magician makes its mountains;
Makes all larger, larger, larger.

III

Into the earth the Magician glances;
Into its mountains he may see.

IV

I have made the Sun!
I have made the Sun!
Hurling it high
In the four directions.
To the East I threw it
To run its appointed course.

V

I have made the Moon!
I have made the Moon!
Hurling it high
In the four directions.
To the East I threw it
To run its appointed course.

VI

I have made the Stars!
    I have made the Stars!
Above the earth I threw them.
    All things above I've made
And placed them to illumine.

WARS OF THE PEOPLE

I

AFTER A TIME ELDER BROTHER WENT WITH THE PEOPLE TO SLAY HÂ-ÂK, THE FEMALE MONSTER

Dazzling power has Elder Brother,
    Mastering the winds with song.
Swiftly now we come together,
    Singing to secure control.
Kovakova, kovakova,
    Kovakova, kovakova.
Singing on the summit
    Of great Mo-hatûk mountain,
Anayokuna, anayokuna, hayokuna.
Sacred pipe of Tcu-unarsat,
    Sleep-inducing sacred pipe,
Anayokuna, anayokuna, hayokuna.
    Hâ-âk flees from her pursuers,
But her spring and mortar stay.
Throw a great stone!
Throw a great stone!
    The blue owl is brightest,
Throw a great stone!
    The blue owl is brightest,
Throw a great stone.

II

WHEN THEY HAD SLAIN HÂ-ÂK THEY WENT AGAINST THEIR ENEMIES, SINGING:

We go; we go; we go; we go.
      Happy, we leave our homes.
We go; happily we go.
We run; we run; we run; we run.
      Happy, we leave our land.
With pleasure hence we hasten.

III

THUS SANG THE PEOPLE AS THEY CAME UP OUT OF THE EARTH, WHITHER THEY FLED DURING THE FLOOD:

Together we emerge with our rattles;
Together we emerge with our rattles,
      Bright-hued feathers in our headdresses.

With our nyñnyirsa we went down,
With our nyñnyirsa we went down;
      Wearing Yoku feathers in our headdresses.

This is the White Land, we arrive singing,
      Headdresses waving in the breeze.
We have come! We have come!
      The land trembles with our dancing and singing.

      We run, we run, we run, we run,
Happy we leave our land;
      With pleasure hence we hasten.

On these Black mountains all are singing,
      Headdresses waving, headdresses waving.

We all rejoice! We all rejoice!
> Singing, dancing, the mountains trembling.

IV

**WHEN THEY ATTACKED THE MEN OF MORNING-BLUE
THEY SANG:**

Yonder stands the doomed habitation.
> About the pueblo runs its frightened chieftain
In yellow garment with hand-print decoration.

V

AT GILA CROSSING ELDER BROTHER SANG:

I am the magician who with the sacred pipe
> Of Tcu-unarsat increase my magic power.
I am the magician of the downy feathers.
> With the soothing sacred pipe
I bring sleep upon my enemy.

VI

**THEY WENT AGAINST THE ENEMY NEAR TEMPE,
SINGING:**

Look for him! Look for him!
> Poor distracted enemy; take him!
Poor fear-stricken enemy; take him!

VII

WHEN HE CLIMBED THE CLIFF TO ATTACK EAGLE, ELDER BROTHER SANG:

Up the cliff, steep and smooth,
    Up the cliff, steep and smooth,
Up the cliff, steep and smooth,
    Climbs Elder Brother
With his shining power.
    Up the cliff, steep and smooth,
Up the cliff, steep and smooth,
    He climbs step by step.

VIII

THERE HE CONCEALED HIMSELF AS A FLY, SINGING:

Himovali! Die fly! Himovali! Die fly!
    I shall sleep! I shall sleep!
Himovali! Let die! I am drowsy.
    I will sleep! Buzz-z.

IX

WHEN EAGLE RETURNED HIS WIFE PUT HIM TO SLEEP WITH THIS SONG:

Haya yakahai yahai mo! Haya yakahai mo!
    I am sleepy, I am sleepy.
Haya yakahai yahai mo! I am sleepy.

X

THEN THE ELDER BROTHER SLEW THE EAGLE AND RETURNING IN TRIUMPH, ELDER BROTHER CELEBRATED HIS PROWESS:

Child of the Raven! Child of the Raven!
     You of the dazzling power.
See my magic power shining like the mirage.

HUNTING SONGS

I

At the time of the White Dawn;
     At the time of the White Dawn,
I arose and went away.
     At Blue Nightfall I went away.

I ate the thornapple leaves
     And the leaves made me dizzy.
I drank thornapple flowers
     And the drink made me stagger.
The hunter, Bow-remaining,
     He overtook and killed me,
Cut and threw my horns away.
     The hunter, Reed-remaining,
He overtook and killed me,
     Cut and threw my feet away.

Now the flies become crazy
     And they drop with flapping wings.
The drunken butterflies sit
     With opening and shutting wings.

II

Young Hare Magician running
    Brings black-tailed deer venison.
And young Badger Magician
    Brings the feet of black-tailed deer.

Had I neither winds or clouds?
    In the east the Yellow Ikol,
In the west the Yellow Ikol
    Called me. I had no winds or clouds.

BASKET-BEATING SONGS

I

As the Sun sinks to the westward
    We begin singing the Eagle songs.
The home of the Magician rises,
    Standing before me in the land.
We begin singing the Eagle songs.

Earth Magician now comes hither;
    Earth Magician now comes hither.
From the depths the songs are rising,
    And by him are here established.
As now the land is prosperous;
    As now the land is prosperous
Elder Brother comes from the East;
    He comes here as a child might,
The land prospers with his coming.

It was in the western mountains
    That White-Eater Woman dwelt.
It was in the western mountains
    That White-Eater Woman dwelt.

The evening glows red in the West,
>> And the birds here gather about me.
Now I hear the screams of the Eagle.
>> Haiya ha aiya haya haya ha-a!
Now I meet and see you. Haiya ha!

II

Roll from cliff end to cliff end,
>> Roll, Winds, from the steep house walls.
Thus the growing excitement
>> Gathers like the winds that blow
From the house of Wind Magician.

In the East, my younger brothers,
>> We are preceded by the bearers
Of the sacred eagle feathers.
>> In the East, my younger brothers,
We are preceded by the bearers
>> Of the sacred eagle feathers

In the distant land of Eagle,
>> In the distant land of Eagle
Sounds the harmonious rolling
>> Of reverberating thunder.

Now the Swallow begins his singing;
>> Now the Swallow begins his singing.
And the women who are with me,
>> The poor women begin to sing.

The Swallows meet in the standing cliffs;
>> The Swallows meet in the standing cliffs.
And the rainbows arched above me,
>> There the blue rainbow arches meet.

The Black Swallows running hither;
>> The Black Swallows running hither,

Running hither come to lead me,
    Lead me there, lead me there.

Haiya! Far in the distant east
    Lie the clouds hidden under the mountain.
Far in the east direction
    To the hidden clouds I come running.

We are beating the basket drums:
    We are beating the basket drums.
I am singing, I am listening;
    From my feathers clouds are shaking.

I am circling like the Vulture,
    Staying, flying near the blue.
I am circling like the Vulture,
    Breathing, flying near the blue.

Now the Reddish Bat rejoices
    In the songs which we are singing;
He rejoices in the eagle down
    With which we ornament our headdress.

I ran into the swamp confused;
    There I heard the Tadpoles singing.
I ran into the swamp confused,
    Where the bark-clothed Tadpoles sang.

In the West the Dragonfly wanders,
    Skimming the surface of the pools,
Touching only with his tail. He skims
    With flapping and rustling wings.

Thence I run as the darkness gathers,
    Wearing cactus flowers in my hair.
Thence I run as the darkness gathers,
    In fluttering darkness to the singing place.

SONG OF THE RACE

Many people have gathered together,
    I am ready to start in the race,
And the Swallow with beating wings
    Cools me in readiness for the word.

Far in the west stands the Black mountain
    Around which our racers ran at noon.
Who is this man running with me,
    The shadow of whose hands I see?

SONG OF STRANGENESS

Singing to the gods in supplication;
    Singing to the gods in supplication,
Thus my magic power is uplifted.
    My power is uplifted as I sing.

Harlots hither running come;
    Harlots hither running come,
Holding blue flowers as they run.
    Talking in whispers they file along.

Along the crooked trail I'm going,
    Along the crooked trail going west.
To the land of rainbows I'm going,
    Swinging my arms as I journey on.

NAME-SONG

The ceremonial reeds are lifted;
    The ceremonial reeds are lifted.
Ma-akahi has killed an Apache,
    And we meet together here in war paint

To collect hair trophies with their power.
      Hivayomi has taken a captive,
And the magic of his bow dies with him.

PUBERTY SONG

Come, hurry forth, hurry forth.
      Already the echoing sounds
Of darkness are heard around.

The Virgin is not sleepy,
She is wakeful through the night.

The Saguaro lies there broken;
      And my fallen feathers rise
O'er the top of Table Mountain.

The boy stirred the rumbling stones;
      The woman heard and could not sleep.
And my toe nails are broken.

The branches of darkness fell,
Cutting my feathers as I passed.

SONG OF THE MAGIC OF DAWN

On the top of Móhatûk
      There are many clouds standing.
On the top of Móhatûk
      Many fog clouds are rising.
The bitter wind blows on us;
      The bitter wind blows on us,
As we sing with many bows.

Though I am a Navitco,
      I hear you talk about me.
I thrust my head through the sky
      And with it I run away.

Cut sticks, cut sticks, cut sticks straight.

FETISH SONG

We commence the fetish song;
      We commence the fetish song.
It is difficult but I try;
      The night grows very noisy.

The fetish song arises;
      The fetish song arises.
To it the crazed women run;
      To it the crazed women run.

Pity me! Oh, pity me!
      And strip away my disease;
Now strip away my disease;
      Clear it away by singing.
I'm going to the singing;
      I'm going to the singing.
It is leading to the mountain,
      Running to Sievat mountain.

LIGHTNING SONG

See the destructive lightning
      Going to kill the distant tree.
It is going, my younger brother,
      To split the distant tree.

Around the mountain I carry
   My poor younger brother:
Carry him around the mountain
   And then stand before it.

The lightning like reddish snakes
   Tries to lash and shiver the trees.
The lightning tries to strike them,
   But it fails and they still stand.

Through the roaring darkness I run,
   Carrying my poor younger brother;
From the top of the sky the lightning
   Shoots, and strikes nearby.

HORNED TOAD SONG

The East Land seems very pleasant.
   I go toward it and I see
How pleasant it seems to be.
   I go toward the Pleasant Land.

West Land is most terrible.
   I go toward it and I see
How terrible the Land is.
   I go toward the fearful Land.

GILA MONSTER SONG

Pitiable harlot though I am,
   My heart glows with the singing
While the evening yet is young.
   My heart glows with the singing.

Where the two stones were standing,
　　　Black Wind roared in fearful blasts,
Driving the birds before him
　　　Fluttering back and forth.

On the summit of white Ngiwolik
　　　There the green frogs are singing.
Lying near the blue storm clouds
　　　There many frogs are singing.

BLACK LIZARD SONG

We first sing at the Magician's;
　　　We first sing at the Magician's,
The round disk of the Sun arose,
　　　Accompanied with its rays.

Harlots came running in a group;
　　　Harlots came running in a group.
Harlots came with hikimoli,
　　　Flower crowns upon their heads.

Black Lizard found the trail where
　　　Elder Brother had been running,
And he came out from the clouds
　　　With water upon his arms.

Darkness settles on the summit
　　　Of the great Stony Mountain.
There circling round it settles
　　　On the great Stony Mountain.

The ruddy beams like spider threads
　　　Across the sky came streaming.
The reddish snakes like spider's web
　　　To the opposite side came flaming.

BLACK-TAILED DEER SONG

Down from the houses of magic;
      Down from the houses of magic,
Blow the winds and from my antlers,
      And my ears they stronger gather.

Over there I ran trembling;
      Over there I ran trembling,
For bows and arrows pursued me.
      Many bows were on my trail.

What horse is trying to catch me?
      What horse is trying to catch me?
The horse with the star forehead
      Now slowly gains upon me.

We are sitting here together;
      We are sitting here together,
Singing the song of the east,
      Singing the song of the west.

RATTLESNAKE SONG

In the early evening,
      In the early evening
We begin to sing many songs;
      And I join in singing many.

It was near Kâ-matûk mountain
      That this Rattlesnake came forth;
And he saw the low clouds lying
      Near the summit of the mountain.

Who is this, who is this?
      Is it not Horned Rattlesnake?

Is it not Horned Rattlesnake
      Who now appears before us?

The Butterflies are singing;
      The Butterflies are singing,
As I go past the foundations
      Below, of the ancient house.

BEAVER SONG

You talk about and fear me;
      You talk about and fear me.
As like the sinuous snake
      I go upon the water.

I see that you go slowly;
      I see that you go slowly.
Strong as the Sun among the trees,
      You leave your mark upon them.

Younger brother, I am Beaver,
      I am the quick-eared Beaver
That gnaws the trees of the forest,
      'Tis I who overthrow them.

OWL SONG

Toward great Kâ-matûk mountain
      I go to join the singing,
During the glow of evening.
      I meet all the singers there.

Owl is singing in the distance,
      I hear him moving back and forth.

Many harlots came here running;
      Here came running and came laughing.

Small Owl resembles Tcokot;
      The winds rise from Owl's feathers.
With their ashy tips he starts them.
      Small Owl is like the Large Owl.

Owl makes me drink the reddish water;
      Rapidly intoxicated
I try to walk straight toward the east,
      And find my footsteps staggering.

QUAIL SONG

The Gray quails were bunched together
      Coyote ran to look upon them.
The Blue quails were bunched together;
      Coyote looked sidewise at them.

MOUSE SONG

Wings of birds invisible
      Are now fluttering above you.
You stand with face uplifted
      And quietly listen there.

Our land was unfortunate;
      The floods came rolling westward,
Then they came flowing westward,
      And I cried out much afraid.

BEAR SONG

I am the Black Bear. Around me
    You see the light clouds extending.
I am the Black Bear. Around me
    You see the light dew falling.

I drink the reddish liquor
    Which kills the spirit in me.
I drink the reddish liquor
    Which kills the spirit in me.

Now the singing has commenced,
    Now the singing has commenced.
I go with my younger brother;
    I know the songs we're singing.

ROADRUNNER SONG

Roadrunner with the bushy head
    Is always crying, poi! poi!
As he runs around the house.
    Poi! poi! around the house.

Here is the lonely Roadrunner;
    Here is the lonely Roadrunner.
He eats lizards in the morning;
    He eats solitary lizards.

Here is the red-eyed Roadrunner;
    Here is the red-eyed Roadrunner,
Who runs about the mistletoe.
    This is the red-eyed Roadrunner.

I run and hide! I run and hide!
    Now I kill the Gray Lizard

And I eat his fat body.
     I run and hide! I run and hide.

Over yonder in the mesquite
     Stands the Hawk's nest with its branches
Which rise like kiâhâ frame sticks,
     Over yonder in the mesquite.

DOG SONG

The songs commence at nightfall,
     And the winds blow toward the north.
The winds are blowing strongly,
     Blowing my tail toward the north.

Butterfly wings are falling;
     Butterfly wings are falling,
Falling upon and harming;
     My suffering is greater.

See the small dogs come running;
     See the poor dogs come running.
See the horsemen coming after;
     See the horsemen come laughing.

HARE SONG

Hare is jumping and singing;
     Hare is jumping and singing,
While the wind is roaring.
     While the wind is roaring.

Hare is dancing and singing;
     Hare is dancing and singing,

While the clouds are roaring,
    While the clouds are roaring.

With headdress of owl feathers;
    With headdress of owl feathers,
He comes to my far country;
    He comes bringing hence his bow.

The Gray Mouse came at nightfall;
    The Gray Mouse came at nightfall,
Came running in the darkness;
    Came breathing in the darkness.

I am shut in at day dawn;
    I am shut in at day dawn,
All night I am free to run
    But am shut in at day dawn.

GOPHER SONG

In the reddish glow of nightfall,
    In the reddish glow of nightfall
I return to my burrow,
    About which the flowers bloom.

With the four eagle feathers,
    With the four eagle feathers
I stir the air. When I turn
    My magic power is crossed.

And I make hills of soft earth;
    And I make hills of soft earth.
My breath withers all before it;
    My breath withers all before it.

COYOTE SONG

Coyote commences singing;
    Coyote commences singing.
The young woman hurries forth
    To hear the Coyote songs.

A hat of eagle feathers;
    A hat of eagle feathers,
A headdress was made for me
    That made my heart grow stronger.

Coyote ran around it;
    Coyote ran around it,
Ran into the blue water,
    Changed the color of his hair.

BADGER SONG

Here am I unfortunate;
    Here am I unfortunate,
Not to know the songs to sing;
    The songs we sing at sunset.

There came a Gray Owl at sunset
    There came a Gray Owl at sunset
Hooting softly around me,
    He brought terror to my heart.

The land lay quietly sleeping;
    The land lay quietly sleeping.
My young stretch, crying, haya!
    Pity them digging in the dust.

You Sun out there in the west;
    You Sun out there in the west,

You are now talking to me.
      You are sounding your gourd rattle.

The land is parched and burning,
      The land is parched and burning.
Going and looking about me
      I see a narrow strip of green.

Yet I do not know surely,
      Yet I do not know surely.
The harlot is here among us.
      I go away toward the west.

The shadow of Crooked mountain,
      The curved and pointed shadow.
'Twas there that I heard the singing;
      Heard the songs that harmed my heart.

The light glow of evening;
      The light glow of evening
Comes as the quails fly slowly,
      And it settles on the young.

BUTTERFLY SONG

The Butterfly song we now commence;
      The Butterfly song we now commence,
Dancing on sides to and fro
      Until the dust arises.

The Butterfly Bird, the Butterfly Bird
      Commences to sing his many songs.
I run to where the dust arises,
      Close to the walls of the house.

I commence the song, I commence the song.
    I heard the singing as I ran;
I heard the singing as I ran.
    I join with the singing.

The Cat-tail Woman commences singing;
    The Cat-tail Woman commences singing.
I join the circling dancers,
    Striking my breast and singing.

I sail in the clouds to Table mountain;
    I sail in the clouds to Table mountain,
And I sing with Kâ-matûk mountain
    Upon which there are no clouds.

Hurry to the Dead Standing mountain;
    Hurry to the Dead Standing mountain.
See there, my Younger Brother,
    How the winds there run their course.

At the clearing of Ma-ayal mountain;
    At the clearing of Ma-ayal mountain,
Before the house of the Magician,
    There stands the woman laughing.

Here on the slopes of Crooked mountain;
    Here on the slopes of Crooked mountain,
Around whose crest the foam remains,
    We have run for blue water.

DEMON SONG

Singing at Kâ-matûk mountain;
    Singing at Kâ-matûk mountain,
I listen to their singing;
    I come running to sing with them.

Evening now is falling;
  Evening now is falling,
And demons appeared running
  To strip and expose my soul.

In a Santa Rita cave;
  In a Santa Rita cave,
As I entered in the cave,
  I saw the breath of demons.

Here demon boys came running;
  Here demon boys came running,
Grasping my hair they carried me,
  Brought me to a distant land.

RAIN SONGS

I

Hi-ihiya naiho-o! Let us begin our song,
  Let us begin, rejoicing. Hitciya yahina-a.
Let us begin our song, let us begin rejoicing,
  Singing of the large corn. Hitciya yahina-a.
Singing of the small corn. Hitciya yahina-a.

II

Hi-ihiya naiho-o! The darkness of evening
  Falls as we sing before the sacred âmina.
About us on all sides corn tassels are waving.
  Hitciya yahina! The white light of day dawn
Yet finds us singing, while corn tassels are waving.
  Hitciya yahina-a! The darkness of evening
Falls as we sing before the sacred âmina.
  About us on all sides corn tassels are waving.
Hitciya yahina! The white light of day dawn
  Yet finds us singing, while the squash leaves are
waving.

Hi-iya naiho-o! The earth is rumbling
       From the beating of our basket drums.
The earth is rumbling from the beating
       Of our basket drums, everywhere humming.
Earth is rumbling, everywhere raining.

III

Hi-ihiya naiho-o! Pluck out the feathers
       From the wing of the Eagle and turn them
Toward the east where lie the large clouds.
       Hitciya yahina-a! Pluck out the soft down
From the breast of the Eagle and turn it
       Toward the west where sail the small clouds.
Hitciya yahina! Beneath the abode
       Of the rain gods it is thundering;
Large corn is there. Hitciya yahina!
       Beneath the abode of the rain gods
It is raining; small corn is there.

WAR SONGS

I

Over that black sandy land,
       Over the top came running,
Over the top came running.
       The Apache slave was killed
And his hide tanned for leather.

II

Here the warrior, Shining-row,
       Came and saw the night around me.
Young Coyote made a shield house
       And he sat in it shouting,
And that was pleasing to me.
       Young Coyote tied the darkness;

The cigarettes were passed around,
        Four times when he led me there.
The Hawk on Mahyal mountain
        Stood with me beating his wings.

III

There arose in the East Land
        One whom I met there smoking
Flowerlike cigarettes.

Running dazed and falsely speaking
        Pitiable and faint-hearted
I feel at Crooked mountain.

There I'm going, there I'm going.
        I have to drink the liquor
That makes me stagger as I run.

Vulture arose from Sandy hill
        Shining upon the land around.

IV

The Gray Spider magician
        He made a square kiâhâ.
He is indeed a magician.

They are shouting, they are shouting,
        Around the hill of Atci.
The poor people there are shouting
        As the news of battle comes.

V

Now where is he, where is he,
        That he has not already come?
Yes, I fear that he has been killed.

You hung the Raven trophies
  On a pole and danced around them.

Amid the rocks of the mountain
  The women tried to hide themselves;
But the men ran and killed them.

CORN SONG

Hi-ilo-o ya-a-a! He who sees everything
  Sees two stalks of corn standing;
He's my younger brother. Hi-ilo-o ya-a-a!
  He who sees everything, sees the two squashes;
He's my younger brother. Hi-ilo-o ya-a-a!
  On the summit of Ta-atûkah sees the corn standing;
He's my younger brother. Hi-ilo-o ya-a-a!
  On the summit of Ta-atûkah sees the squash standing;
He's my younger brother. Hi-ilo-o woiha!

Hi-ilo-o ya-a-a! Over Ta-atûkam
  Rise the clouds with their loud thundering.
Hi-ilo-o ya-a-a! Over Ta-atûkam
  Rise the clouds with their loud raining.
Hi-ilo-o ya-a-a! The Bluebird is holding
  In his talons the clouds that are thundering.
Hi-ilo-o ya-a-a! Yellowbird is holding
  In his talons the clouds that are raining.

Hi-ilo-o ya-a-a! See Elder Brother
  Breathe out the winds that over Ta-atûkam
Drive the clouds with their loud thundering.
Hi-ilo-o ya-a-a! See Elder Brother
  Breathe out the winds that over Ta-atûkam
  The welcome storm clouds are suspending.
Hi-ilo-o ya-a-a! In the great rain clouds
  Let me sing my song of rejoicing.

MAGICIAN SONG

At early dawn I entered,
       Entered in the white light of day.
And my heart flamed with power
       As I entered the magic house.

In the lofty feather house
       His magic is increasing,
And he moves very slowly
       With the power in his heart.

Elder Brother first came forth;
       Elder Brother first came forth,
And with his shining power
       Governed over all the land.

Earth Magician became angry;
       Earth Magician became angry,
And with his magic power
       He destroyed all the houses.

With a Black Snake I tie them;
       With a Black Snake I tie them,
The houses with a Black Snake,
       The houses with a Black Snake.

With a White Snake I tie them;
       With a White Snake I tie them,
The houses with a White Snake,
       The houses with a White Snake.

NAVITCO SONG

The chicken beans are rattling,
       They are rattling as they fall.

The chicken beans are rattling,
> They are rattling as they fall.

And the stone wall arose there,
> And the stone wall arose there.
When the gourd seed was planted
> It made its way through to grow.

WIND SONG

Wind now commences to sing;
> Wind now commences to sing.
The land stretches before me,
> Before me stretches away.

Wind's house now is thundering;
> Wind's house now is thundering.
I go roaring o'er the land,
> The land covered with thunder.

Over the windy mountains;
> Over the windy mountains,
Came the myriad-legged wind;
> The wind came running hither.

The Black Snake Wind came to me;
> The Black Snake Wind came to me,
Came and wrapped itself about,
> Came here running with its song.

Swiftly with a cup of water
> I came running to make you drink.
I make you drink the water
> And turn dizzily around.

Among the white cactus leaves;
       Among the white cactus leaves,
I came running to that place;
       I came running to that place.

SONG OF THE VISION-MAKER

The evening glow yet lingers;
       The evening glow yet lingers,
And I sit with my gourd rattle
       Engaged in the sacred chant.
As I wave the eagle feathers
       We hear the magic sounding.

Puissant Night is shaking me
       Just as he did at the time
When I was taken up in spirit
       To the great Magician's house.

Yellow Bird placed his feathers
       Where they fell on the head of the woman;
Making of her a harlot who ran about
       With her hands clasped before her.

Bluebird drifted at the edge of the world,
       Drifted along upon the blue wind.
White Wind went down from his dwelling
       And raised dust upon the earth.

The moonshine abides in me;
       And soon you men and women will see
The reed that I now am blowing
       Bring the Moon down to meet me.

Haiya! The gourd is rattling;
       Haiya! The gourd is rattling.

When I go to see it there
    I surely find it rattling.

It is evening, it is evening.
    And four times at evening
Calls the white-headed Swallow
    As he plucks out his feathers.

Elder Brother cuts his reed,
    Yonder before me now he throws it,
Stepping upon it so that the
    Clouds repeat the sound.

Gray Coyote is a dirty meddler,
    He wears a belt of snake skin.
Gray Coyote is a dirty meddler,
    He wears a belt of snake skin.

Blue Frog-women met and carried me
    To the cloud land in the East.
Blue Frog-women met and carried me
    To where the clouds are standing.

Gray Coyote stood in the forest,
    From his shoulders he plucked feathers
That gave me shining power,
    Plucked wing feathers bearing power.

I entered Yâinupanu mountain
    And saw Elder Brother's land
Marked off with its square corners,
    Marked as in a rectangle.

Yellow Bird carries me to the caves,
    To the distant caves of the mountain,
And we hear the sound of his footsteps
    As he moves upon his way.

Gray Road-runner, the magician,
    As his young cried out with hunger,
Ran about engaged in killing
    Millipeds that he carried home.

The Black Turtle now approaches us,
    Wearing and shaking his belt of night.
The Black Turtle now approaches us,
    Wearing and shaking his belt of night.

The harlot arose and ran about,
    Beating her breast and the air.
The harlot arose and ran about,
    Beating her breast and the air.

Understand, my younger brothers,
    That it is the Sun that gives me
The trance vision that I see.
    The Sun gives magic power.

NOTE

"Tell me," I asked an Indian song-poet who had just taught me a song of his composing, "when you made your song, which came first, words or music?"

The Indian stared at me in puzzled surprise: "I made a song," he answered, "a song *is* words and music—all comes together."

Because Indian poems are therefore really songs, conceived as a very part of the iteration and intonation of music, I have endeavored in my translations to hold in minutest detail to the original rhythm and accent, believing that only thus can the Indian verse sing, through an alien tongue, in its true form.

NATALIE CURTIS
Santa Fe, New Mexico, September, 1917

SONG OF THE EARTH
NAVAJO

All is beautiful,
All is beautiful,
All is beautiful, indeed.

Now the Mother Earth
And the Father Sky,
    Meeting, joining one another,
    Helpmates ever, they.
    All is beautiful,
    All is beautiful,
    All is beautiful, indeed.

Sisnajinni,
Tsodsichl,
    Meeting, joining one another,
    Helpmates ever, they.
    All is beautiful,
    All is beautiful,
    All is beautiful, indeed.

Now Doko-oslid
And Depenitsa,
    Meeting, joining one another,
    Helpmates ever, they.
    All is beautiful,
    All is beautiful,
    All is beautiful, indeed.

And the night of darkness
And the dawn of light,
    Meeting, joining one another,
    Helpmates ever, they.
    All is beautiful,
    All is beautiful,

All is beautiful, indeed.

Now Hastyeyalli
And Hastyehogan,
    Meeting, joining one another,
    Helpmates ever, they.
      All is beautiful,
      All is beautiful,
      All is beautiful, indeed.

And the white corn
And the yellow corn,
    Meeting, joining one another,
    Helpmates ever, they.
      All is beautiful,
      All is beautiful,
      All is beautiful, indeed.

And the corn-pollen
And the Ripener,
    Meeting, joining one another,
    Helpmates ever, they.
      All is beautiful,
      All is beautiful,
      All is beautiful, indeed.

Life-that-never-passeth,
Happiness-of-all-things,
    Meeting, joining one another,
    Helpmates ever, they.
      All is beautiful,
      All is beautiful,
      All is beautiful, indeed.

      Now all is beautiful,
      All is beautiful,
      All is beautiful, indeed.

HUNTING SONG
NAVAJO

Comes the deer to my singing,
Comes the deer to my song,
Comes the deer to my singing.

He, the blackbird, he am I,
Bird beloved of the wild deer,
Comes the deer to my singing.

From the Mountain Black,
From the summit,
Down the trail, coming, coming now,
Comes the deer to my singing.

Through the blossoms,
Through the flowers, coming, coming now,
Comes the deer to my singing.

Through the flower dew-drops,
Coming, coming now,
Comes the deer to my singing.

Through the pollen, flower pollen,
Coming, coming now,
Comes the deer to my singing.

Starting with his left fore-foot,
Stamping, turns the frightened deer,
Comes the deer to my singing.

Quarry mine, blessed am I
In the luck of the chase.
Comes the deer to my singing.

Comes the deer to my singing,
Comes the deer to my song,
Comes the deer to my singing.

SONG OF THE RAIN CHANT
NAVAJO

Far as man can see,
    Comes the rain,
    Comes the rain with me.

From the Rain-Mount,
Rain-Mount far away,
    Comes the rain,
    Comes the rain with me.

O'er the corn,
O'er the corn, tall corn,
    Comes the rain,
    Comes the rain with me.

'Mid the lightnings,
'Mid the lightnings zigzag,
'Mid the lightnings flashing,
    Comes the rain,
    Comes the rain with me.

'Mid the swallows,
'Mid the swallows blue,
Chirping glad together,
    Comes the rain,
    Comes the rain with me.

Through the pollen,
Through the pollen blest,
All in pollen hidden,
    Comes the rain,
    Comes the rain with me.

Far as man can see,
    Comes the rain,
    Comes the rain with me.

SONG FROM THE MOUNTAIN CHANT
NAVAJO

Thereof he telleth.

Now of the Holy Youth,
Thereof he telleth.

Moccasins decked with black,
Thereof he telleth.

And richly broidered dress,
Thereof he telleth.

Arm-bands of eagle feathers,
Thereof he telleth.

And now the rain-plumes,
Thereof he telleth.

Now of the Male-Rain,
Thereof he telleth.

Now of the rain-drops fallen,
Thereof he telleth.

Now of Unending Life,
Thereof he telleth.

Now of Unchanging Joy,
Thereof he telleth.

Thereof he telleth.

CORN-GRINDING SONG
ZUÑI

I

O, my lovely mountain,
    To' yallanne!
O, my lovely mountain,
    To' yallanne!
    To' yallanne!
High up in the sky,
See Rain-makers seated,
Hither come the rain-clouds now,
    He-ya, ha-ya, he-ya!

Behold, yonder
All will soon be abloom
Where the flowers spring—
Tall shall grow the youthful corn-plants.

II

Lovely! See the cloud, the cloud appear!
Lovely! See the rain, the rain draw near!
    Who spoke?
'Twas the little corn-ear
High on the tip of the stalk
Singing while it looked at me
    Talking aloft there—
"Ah, perchance the floods
    Hither moving—
Ah, may the floods come this way!"

III

Yonder, yonder the fair rainbow,
See the rainbow brightly decked and painted!
Now the swallow bringeth glad news to your corn,

Singing, "Hitherward, hitherward, hitherward, rain,
    "Hither come!
    "Hither come!"
Now hear the corn-plants murmur,
"We are growing, everywhere!
"Hi, yai! The world, how fair!"

KOROSTA KATZINA SONG
HOPI

    Yellow butterflies,
Over the blossoming virgin corn,
    With pollen-painted faces
Chase one another in brilliant throng.

    Blue butterflies,
Over the blossoming virgin beans,
    With pollen-painted faces
Chase one another in brilliant streams.

    Over the blossoming corn,
    Over the virgin corn
Wild bees hum!

    Over the blossoming beans,
    Over the virgin beans
Wild bees hum!

Over your field of growing corn
    All day shall hang the thunder-cloud;
Over your field of growing corn
    All day shall come the rushing rain.

HE-HEA KATZINA SONG
HOPI

Corn-blossom maidens
Here in the fields,
Patches of beans in flower,
Fields all abloom,
Water shining after rain,
Blue clouds looming above.

Now behold!
Through bright clusters of flowers
Yellow butterflies
Are chasing at play,
And through the blossoming beans
Blue butterflies
Are chasing at play.

SONGS FROM

CALIFORNIA

SONGS OF SPIRITS
WINTU

I

LIGHTNING

I bear the sucker-torch to the western tree-ridge.
Behold me! first born and greatest.

II

OLELBIS (THE CREATOR)

I am great above.
I tan the black cloud.

III

HAU (RED FOX)

On the stone ridge east I go.
On the white road I, Hau, crouching go.
I, Hau, whistle on the road of stars.

IV

POLAR STAR

The circuit of earth which you see,
The scattering of stars in the sky which you see,
All that is the place for my hair.

SONGS OF KUMASTAMXO
YUMA

I

WHEN THE SPIRIT-WIND APPROACHED

"The Wind is wandering, is wandering;
The Wind is wandering, is wandering."

II

WHEN HE BURNT THE UNCLEAN HOUSE

"The house will burn, will burn.
The house will be crackling, will be crackling.
It will blaze.
We are going to dance.
It is going to be lighted.
It is going to be lighted.
It will blaze.
We are going to dance.
Something bird-like is coming.*

Bird-like tracks will be about the place.
We are going to light this unclean house.
It will blaze, blaze."

III

WHEN HE MADE THE RIVER

"This is my water, my water.
This is my river, my river.
We love its water.

---

*Where a house had been burnt seeds were scattered, for the birds to
devour.

We love its foamwood.
It shall flow forever.
It shall flow forever.
When the weather grows hot, it shall rise and overflow
    its banks.
It shall flow forever."

IV

AFTER HE HAD FINISHED HIS CREATING

"Into the earth I go down, go down.
Nothing but earth will I be seeing, will I be seeing.
I sink down into the old river-bed,
Down into the interior."

V

WHEN HE BECAME THE EAGLE

"I am springing, springing.
Wing-feathers!
Body-feathers!
On my hands wing-feathers.
On my body body-feathers."

SONGS FROM
THE NORTHWEST COAST

PRAYERS OF THE TSIMSHIAN TO NEXNÓX

Nexnóx, Nexnóx!
Chief, Chief!
    have pity upon us!
    else there will be nobody
    to smoke under you!
Nexnóx, have pity upon us!

FOR FAIR WEATHER

Nexnóx, Nexnóx!
Chief, Chief!
    have pity upon us!
Look down and see
    what those under you
    whom you made are doing!
Pull up your foot
    and sweep off your face!*

FOR CALM WEATHER

Hold in your breath, Chief,
    that it may be calm.

---

*"Pull up your foot" means "stop the rain"; "sweep off your face" means "take away the clouds."

THREE SONGS FROM THE HAIDA: QUEEN CHARLOTTE'S ISLAND, B.C.

LOVE SONG

Beautiful is she, this woman,
As the mountain flower;
But cold, cold, is she,
Like the snowbank
Behind which it blooms.

THE BEAR'S SONG

(Whoever can sing this song is admitted forever to the friendship of the bears)

I have taken the woman of beauty
For my wife;
I have taken her from her friends.
I hope her kinsmen will not come
And take her away from me.
I will be kind to her.
Berries, berries I will give her from the hill
And roots from the ground.
I will do everything to please her.
For her I made this song and for her I sing it.

SONG FOR FINE WEATHER

O good Sun,
Look thou down upon us:
Shine, shine on us, O Sun,
Gather up the clouds, wet, black, under thy arms—
That the rains may cease to fall.
Because thy friends are all here on the beach

Ready to go fishing—
Ready for the hunt.
Therefore look kindly on us, O Good Sun!
Give us peace within our tribe
And with all our enemies.
Again, again, we call—
Hear us, hear us, O Good Sun!

BEAR SONG

HAIDA

Chief, chief, that I am,
Be careful how you pull your grandfather around.
Be careful how you pull around your grandfather
As you sit beside him.
I am too much of a boy for you.
Chief, chief that I am,

Chief, chief that I am,
I am already far away.
At the cliff, coming from my passage through the mountains,
I hold up my head grandly.
Chief, chief that I am,
I am already far away from it.
From my blue mountain I am now far away.
On the Island I travel, led about proudly.
From it I am far away.
Chief, chief that I am.

Chief, chief that I am,
They say that I have green mountains.
They say that I went into the creek I own which stretches its
    length afar.
Chief, chief that I am.

Chief, chief that I am,
When the sun rises I start traveling about.
Now I am lying under a deadfall.
Chief, chief that I am.

Chief, chief that I am,
My power is all taken away,
My power is all taken away.
Chief, chief that I am,
My power is all taken away,
Chief, chief that I am.

Chief, chief, whither did my great brother wander proudly?
My mind shakes as I go about.
Chief, chief.

Chief, chief,
Tell me where he fell.
I do not know the place.
Chief, chief, chief.

HAIDA CRADLE SONGS

I

Again perhaps you expect to sit up high in your father's
    canoe*
        chief-woman, and look around upon all things
        in front of Upset-Canoe.
Be careful, be careful, chief-woman!

---

*Chiefs' children used to be placed high up on blankets in the center of
trading canoes so that they could look about. Here the baby is reminded
of what she used to do in a former existence.

Again perhaps you expect to sit up high in your father's
    canoe,

       chief-woman, and look around the place
       whence abalones come.
Be careful, be careful, chief-woman.

II

Perhaps you are crying and crawling
    to get your grandmother's hand
    which was hurt on a wooden tray with square sides, I
       hear;
    for that you are crying and crawling
    chief-woman, chief-woman,
    crying and crawling.

III

    Whence have you fallen, have you fallen?
    Whence have you fallen, have you fallen?
    Did you fall, fall, fall, fall,
        from the top of a salmonberry bush?

IV

Stop crying, chief's child! Stop crying, chief's child!
I do not expect that drums will sound again for you, chief's
    child, if it is for that you are crying and wriggling.
Stop crying, great chief's child, a child of noble family sits
    quietly.
Now, now, great chief's child; a child of noble family sits
    quietly.
Stop crying, chief's child! Stop crying, chief's child!
I do not expect that they are going to lay heavy planks for
    you again, chief's child; if it is for that you are crying and
    wriggling.
Stop crying, great chief's child, a child of noble family sits
    quietly.
Now, now, great chief's child; a child of noble family sits
    quietly.

V

One sits here like a common person facing the woods.
Say, stop telling lies!
Your mouth will be crooked
    you mosquito-people-trash!

VI

In your father's house, your father's house
    Cape Qóna seagulls eating things
    are making cries.
In the midst of all these things
    you are going to move
    proudly as you sit.

VII

Come, let us take it on our knees!
    Come, let us take it on our knees!
Hand it to one another inside of its father's house,
    hand it to one another!
Come, let us take it on our knees!
    Come, let us take it on our knees!

VIII

At that time when my child
    goes about as a youth
    vainly alone
    I shall sit around.
His son
    making a great noise
    went by on the water.
I wonder where he is going!
His son
    making a great noise
    went by on the water.
It must be to the North islands.

IX

Did you make up your mind
    to fall into the cradle
    to fall into the cradle
    to fall in from the top of a spruce-tree?
    to fall in from the top of a salmonberry bush?

X

Be careful, my noble sons!
    you will grow to one another like leaves.
Be careful, my own chief!
    Be careful, my own chief!

XI

Are you crying for this, chief?
Are you crying for this, chief?
Are you crying to have your sisters
    put you up higher, chief?
Crying for your cousins to make the people
    as numerous in front of you
    as when people make seagulls cry,
    being obliged to step on them,—
For these things are you crying, chief?

XII

You came to me, you came to me, ye he he!
You came to me, you came to me.
You came walking to me, calling me "mother,"
    instead of to someone else.
To me my child, who is a chief's child,
    came walking, calling me "mother,"
Mother of noble family,
Mother of noble family, mother of noble family,
    mother of noble family, mother of noble family.

XIII

Why does he cry softly?
Why does he wriggle as he sits?
He wriggles and cries for grandfather's house.

XIV

It is not now as it was in olden times.
Even slaves are beginning to own good abalone-shells!

XV

Dogs, even,
　　　　when they have pups
　　　　to them give their love.
That is why
　　　　mine I love.

XVI

Still stands
　　　　Skîlsîs town.
Do not cry
　　　　upon my knees!

XVII

Why is it
　　　　your slave close by
　　　　(even I, your mother!)
　　　　you want something you cannot get, you say?
You are very foolish,
　　　　uncle reborn,
　　　　I bore.

XVIII

My child says:
　　　　Look around at the waves,—
Then she fools me
　　　　with unripe salmonberries.

XIX

Behind Sea-Lion Town
    I was looking around a while;
    the future chief I found,
    just big enough to walk.
Take care, take care, my own chief!
Take care, my own master!

XX

Women are better than men,
    women are better than men.
Women have more property.
Chiefs of my family,
    where are you?

XXI

    Upon his grandmother's land
        my child walks proudly.
    For that his foot is dear.
    Do not cry!

BILQULA DEATH SONG

    He makes me pure
    O making pure, making pure!
    I destroy not life
    I am the life maker.

SONG OF QAQATCGUK
TLINGIT

The man who thought he had perished
    dreams thus about himself:
    I keep feeling
    as if I had gotten home.

SONG OF WOMAN'S PREMONITION

Already I am going,
           I am going to die.
I have dreamed of my son.

SONG OF RAVEN

That Raven must have been a great fellow.
He went down under the sea.
Then they pulled up his nose.
He went through the town for his nose.
When it was given him he started to fly out of doors.
He flew out with it.
Why! instead of looking like himself, he looks as if he ought
    to have a drink.
After you have done as he has done you can wander about the
    entire world-beach.

CRADLE SONG FOR A GIRL

If I do not take anything to the party
           I shall be ashamed,
           I shall be ashamed.
Little girls, listen.
Little girls, listen.

CRADLE SONG

Let me shoot a small bird
           for my younger brother.
Let me spear a small trout
           for my younger sister.

SONG OF LITTLE-LAKE-UP-ABOVE

(When his people expected others to come with food to give them a feast)

It is before my face every day.
And when I sleep I always think of you.
I long much for you.
Thinking about you comes to me
      like a sudden sickness.

SONG OF SORROW

(By a woman whose brothers were drowned and their bodies not recovered)

Your reef has beaten me,
      Kágwantan's children.
But take pity on me.
I wonder what I always attend to
      when I wake up in the morning.
Sometime I might see my brothers.

COMPOSED BY SMALL-LAKE-UNDERNEATH

(About a drifting log found full of nails, out of which a house was built. Sung when a feast is about to be given for a dead man)

I always compare you to a drifting log
      with iron nails in it.
Let my brother float in,
      in that way.
Let him float ashore
      on a good sandy beach.
I always compare you, my mother,
      to the sun passing behind the clouds.
That is what makes the world dark.

KAGWANTAN SONG FOR THE FEAST

(When a slave is to be killed)
The words of people
> now snow me under,
> the words of worthless people.

SUNG BY THE WOLF FAMILIES

(Coming to a feast)
A rich man is coming.
Your feelings you keep silent.
When it is ended,
> thus they always say:
> "It is all gone."

AT A GREAT FEAST

We are also going to be invited
> to Killisnoo.
High-cast people
> are going to eat.

BY NAQUALI

I wonder what my future life
> will do to me.

SONG OF FOR-A-TOWN SPIRIT

(About the Táqdentan, because when the latter came to Juneau to drink they did not pay any attention to the Auk people.)

I observe how people are treated
after they are dead,
and therefore I drink
before I die.
What you did was very selfish,
Táqdentan's children.
But I do not blame you
for your words.
It is this Raven's fault.

BY NIGOT

What do you think I live for?
I live to drink whiskey.
Have pity on me,
foam children.

BY TSAKAK

It is only crying about myself
that comes to me in song.

BY ONE OF THE LENÉDI

(About Juneau when gold was first found there)

Do not talk any more,
Lenédi's children.
You are ahead
of all the people in the world.

AN ANGRY SONG COMPOSED BY SEXDAGWET

(Against Little Raven, a blind man of Tongas)
Just as if a man chased him
      out on the beach
      because of someone's talking,
      Little Raven threw himself
      before my words.
I do not feel even a little numb.
That fellow, Little Raven,
      whose words
      they are always reporting to me,
      can not see anything.

(On the same subject)
Little Raven,
      I hate what you keep saying,
      because you are a slave's son
      and can see nothing.
I hate to have you talk to me
      because you have spots all over your face
      like a big sea cucumber
      and look like a slave.
Don't you know that,
      because you can not see anything,
      you big slave's son,
      you keep picking up sand
      instead of dipping into the dish?

BY DEAD-SLAVE

(About a woman named Poor-orphan, who was a very poor girl, but afterward became the richest woman in Wrangell)
      I used to make fun
            of this poor little girl at Wrangell
            when she was very small.

BY A SHAMAN OF THE KÁGWANTAN NAMED KAGANK

It is only on account of Strong Drink
    that you pity me.
Why don't you also love me?

BY UNDER-A-BLANKET

(About the son of Luknaxádi, whose brother was killed in compensation for the killing of her brother)
His mind is just like mine,
        Lubnaxádi's children.
So that I am beginning to love him.
I wonder what I always look for
        when I wake up in the morning.
Sometime I might see my brothers.

BY MAN-THAT-IS-NOT-ALL-RIGHT

(About Princess Thom)
Even from a house of Strong Drink
men get away,
but not from you,
Raven woman.

BY AMONG-THE-BRANT

(When his wife had been taken from him)
Like one who desires Strong Drink,
        I never sleep,
        Toqyédi's children.

(On the same subject)
My own mind is very hard to me.
It is just as if
      I were carrying my mind around.
What is the matter with you?

BY OTHER-WATER

(Over a dead man)
My younger brother has brought me
      great joy of laughter.
If I knew the way they go,
      I would go right to him.

BY JOINED-TOGETHER

(When all his friends went down the rapids at Gonaxó and were drowned)
I always look expectantly
      to see some one
      stand up in front of the town
      and in the bay.
I always compare my brothers
      to the people the duck tribe saved.
They went right down under the earth
      like those high-cast people.

BY HERE-IS-A-FEATHER

(When his brother died)
It is as if my grandfather's house
      were turning over with me.
Where is the person who will save me?

BY MAN-FOR-HIMSELF

I love you from my heart,
　　Tsaguédi's children.
You are the only one
　　I will die with.

BY CGWATC

(About an uncle who had died)
I always think within myself
　　that there is no place
　　where people do not die.

MOURNING SONG OF SAKWET

(About her brother who was drowned)
I am like the people
　　who were killed
　　by the south wind.

(On the same subject)
Perhaps my brother went
　　into the sun's trail
　　so that I can never see him again.

PEACE-SONG AFTER A GREAT WAR

If you had died,
　　Kágwantan's children,
　　I would have cut off my hair for you
I love you so much
　　I would have blackened my face for you,
　　Kágwantan's children.

SONG OF A HUMMING-BIRD DEER

I am feeling very lonely away.
I am going to my uncle's town.
I am singing inside, my masters.
I am crying about myself.

BY LQENA

*(When he was the only one of his people saved and his enemies
wanted to make peace with him. He danced as a deer, singing this
song and at the end of it cut in two the man standing next to him)*
I did this way regarding myself.
I would not let what my conscience
        said to me, pass.
Before his death I saw his ghost.
At once he stabbed
        and killed Cadasíktc.

BY QAUCTE

(Who married a Téqoedi woman)
After you have been drinking
        you had better stop talking
        about how well you were brought up,
Téqoedi's children.
What one of you thinks about it.
        when he is sober?

LOVE SONG OF A TAGISH WOMAN

Why have I come to you
    to Dyea from far inland
    only to find
    that you have gone away?
Here I am,
    crying for you.

LOVE-SONG OF SIQUET, THE DANCER

I wonder what this coming July morning
    will be like.
My mind is very weak
    thinking that I shall be unable
    to see my sweetheart.

BY RAVEN-SKIN

(When his sweetheart abandoned him)
If one had control of death
    it would be very easy
    to die with a Wolf woman.
It would be very pleasant.

MOURNING-SONG OF THE KÁGWANTAN

It is his own fault
    that this man of the Wolf people died.
Do not lay the blame on anyone else.

SPELL SONG
KWAKIUTL

What of olden times,
    shall I tell you of olden times
    what of olden times
    my grandchildren?
You of olden times,
    you of olden times,
    a cloud,
    lay on the mountains.

CHINOOK SONGS

SONGS OF THE MAN

I

Ya, that is good!
Ya, that is good!
That worthless woman
    does not like me.

II

Very unhappy I was
    with my wife,
    in Victoria.
Nobody
    said good-day to us
    in Victoria.

III

Aya, aya!
    I have seen
    Sitka your country.
Never mind, if I die
    now soon.

SONGS OF THE WOMAN

I

I don't care
    if you desert me.
Many pretty boys are in the town.
Soon I shall take another one.
That is not hard for me!

II

Nothing shall bother my mind now.
Don't speak to me. I wish I were dead with my sister.

III

    Ya ya,
    When you take a wife,
    Ya ya,
    Don't become angry with me.
    I do not care.

IV

I am very glad
    when the steamboat comes here.
I think I shall cry
    when the steamboat leaves.

V

    I broke down! my dear!
    Say good-bye!
        to me now.
    Always I cry
        for I live far away.

SONGS FROM

THE FAR NORTH

SONGS FOR THE GREAT FEAST TO THE DEAD

I

For our children are gone,
    While those of our friends remain.
       Ai-ya-ya-yai.
Come back, nephew, come back, we miss you;
       Ai-ya-ya-yai.
Come back to us, our lost ones,
    We have presents for you.
       Ai-ya-ya-yai.
Oh, my brother, come back to me,
       Ai-ya-ya-yai.
Come back, my brother, I am lonely,
       Ai-ya-ya-yai.
My brother come back and we
    Will give you a small present,
       Ai-ya-ya-yai-yae-yai, etc.
My children, where are you?
       Ai-ya-ya-yai.
Come back to us, our children.
    We are lonely and sad.
       Ai-ya-ya-yai.

II

    Come, my brother,
    Return to us again;
    We wait for you;

Come, brother, come.
>*Ai-ya-ya-yai.*
Return once more.
Our mother, come back to us.
>*Ai-ya-ya-yai.*
Return, our father;
We wait for you;
Come back to us,
And we, who are lonely,
Will give you food.
>*Ai-ya-ya-yai.*

III

Dead ones, come here;
>*A-la'-ai-ya'*
Come here, do.
>sealskins for a tent you will get,
>*A-la'-ai-ya'*
Come here, do.
>reindeer skins for a bed you will get,
>*A-la'-ai-ya'*

IV

We will sing a song.
We will go down the current.
The waves will rise;
The waves will fall.
The dogs will growl at us.

ESKIMO SONGS

OXAITOQ'S SONG

I walk so long thus
      inland, inland.
I walk so long thus
      inland, inland, and inland.
I am not loved
      inland, inland.
I am not loved
      she is the greatest of all
      inland and inland.
They love best
      inland, inland.
They love best
      what I obtain
      inland and inland.
They love best
      inland, inland.
They love best
      the food that I bring
      inland and inland.

SUMMER SONG

Ajaja, it is pleasant,
      it is pleasant at last
      the great world
      when it is summer at last.
Ajaja, it is pleasant,
      it is pleasant at last
      the great world
      when our caribous begin to come.
Ajaja, they make great noise,

they make great noise,
the brooks there in our country
when it is summer.
Ajaja, this great water
has spread over the ice;
I cannot walk
to the rock across there.
Ajaja, I feel sorry for them,
I feel sorry for them,
not being able to speak,
these gulls.
Ajaja, I feel sorry for them,
I feel sorry for them,
not being able to speak,
these ravens.
A great animal comes now;
no one observes it;
I keep it secret;
the ravens do not tell.
Food like that I cannot obtain.
but quickly I got
little sculpins.
Ajaja, he has found a smooth slope,
he has found a smooth slope,
to burrow into,
the bad old fox.

SEDNOR AND THE FULMAR

AN ESKIMO BALLAD

(Recitative)
Where is she
who would never marry?
In a kayok to the mainland
going away.

Dost thou see, my eyes,
        dost thou see them?
Ia, ha, ha, ha, ha!
To a tent of ragged skins,
        he has brought her, crying;
        (the Fulmar, her husband)
Her father with her elder brother
        in a boat coming;
        (he, seeking his daughter)
In a boat his daughter embarked.
Her husband, the Fulmar, cried:
        (thus the Magician!)
The Fulmar says: "My means for transforming
        let me see them as they are;
        let me see them once more."
Now they are taking the woman back;
        to the tent going home;
        the Fulmar followed,
        (thus the Magician!)
Wind very strong to come near them;
        (he made, the Magician!)
        they were shipwrecked, nearly.
        (Her father fears death!)
His daughter he pushes
        into the sea.
To the boat on both sides—
        to the boat she clings.
        (Still followed, the Fulmar!)
With a knife he struck her;
        whales emerged.
Again he struck her;
        a thong seal emerged.
Again he struck her;
        a fiord seal emerged.
        (thus the Magician!)
Her whole body she leaned.
        (Sednor, fearing death!)

With a knife into the eyes
      he stabbed her;
He killed her.
      (Thus the Fulmar, the Magician!)
On the shore
      her father lifted her.
A quilt he took;
      on the beach laid her down.
With a dog skin she was covered,
      (Sednor, the Beautiful!)
The flood-tide took her.

(Based on a literal translation.)

INTERPRETATIONS

SUMMER DAWN
TEM-EYOS-KYI

She comes—Tem-Eyos-Kwi—
The maiden who has known love!
Last Night Love touched her in the house of waiting.
Love hid the seeds of life in her garments.
In the wind of her walking they are scattered;
All the sod will bloom with them!
None shall be lost: because of her gladness, the gladness of
    love known.

Ah—hi-i! She sees the earth not as we see it—
We who were not overtaken by Love in the house of waiting.

Wake, women, maidens and wives!
Greet Tem-Eyos-Kwi!
Greet her with feet dancing,
With songs of the heart and lips trembling to silence,
Hands that lift their wonder to the breast
Yet touch not the flesh.

Wake, sons, lovers, young chiefs, hunters with
    arrows!
Sharpen the darts, make strong, bend the bow;
Keen, keen as light, and clear as the wind be your eyes!
The women await you in secret places,
They have hidden themselves in the leafy shelters:
All the green leagues of the forest are ashake with invitation.

The quick beating of their hearts is the whisper along the
    bending grass.
The sod grows warm—O men, Summer-dawn is the spirit of
    the women!

        They have washed their hearts with prayer,
And their bodies with juices of cedar:
Perfumed and dried by the wind they have come up from the
    shore—
The great hosts of the women—
Unwrapping themselves from the mists of the morning.
They have entered the forest with the footfalls of muted
    music,
With light tossing steps like the spray on long beaches.
The swinging trees drip dew:
With lines of sparkling rain they point the way the women
    have gone,
Leaving all the paths to them open.

Harken! They follow Tem-Eyos-Kwi, singing:

        "Come, come, O swift and strong!
We are the women: seek us!
Our hearts, like little swallows, nest above the secret pools.
Oh, say, shall not the winged dart pierce,
And the shadow of the bended bow
Stir the still, deep pools?
Oh, the waters shall sparkle and leap and mingle,
And brim at your lips, O men!
They shall be poured out and drip upon a chief's feet;
They shall fill the hollows of his house with children!
Flowing in laughter and whispers and little cries
As smoke through the smoke-hole at evening!
Ai! ah! ai! Women! Waken the soil with freshets;
Bear joy upward as a canoe with sails, swifter than paddles.
O men, hunters of life,

We are the harborers, the fosterers—the women:
Seek us!"

It was the women, the harborers, the fosterers, who rose first,
And followed Tem-Eyos-Kwi:
They called to the men.

  The men go forth like one!
Lightning and heat are their weapons, hurled crashing before
    them.
Their hairs, spreading wide, give black wings to the sun,
As a cloud filled with eagles blown up from the sea.
They enter the forest with the tramp of thunder and the
    darkness of storm;
And the song of the women is stilled.
The cry of offering ascends, it passes the swooping shadows;
There is a sigh through the forest of winds sinking—
Then the hush.

  On the leaves is a sweet whisper of rain,
Whispered sweetness of pangs past.
The warm soil drinks the coolness of tears—
Tears that are dropping melodies
Because cunning hands and strong have shaken the living
    cords.
The skies part, the black wings fold;
The Sun-chief's canoe rides on the upper blue with furled sails:
Tem-Eyos-Kwi, laughing, is at the paddle.
Our village is drenched with light.
(Ei-i! Tem-Eyos-Kwi is glad because Love has overtaken us;
Because now we see the earth as she sees it.)
Two by two, they come up from the forest—the men and the
    women.
The women's smiles are the little sun-tipped clouds
Floating across the face of the mountain:
The look in their eyes is deeper than seas.

High in the light the men lift their heads.
On their clear brows is the mystic mark
Of those from whom a great dream has gone forth.
Firmly they hold the hands of the women,
Who have given peace to their strength, and a meaning.
Together, together, the race-makers enter the lodges.

SONG OF THE SEARCH

I descend through the forest alone.
Rose-flushed are the willows, stark and a-quiver,
In the warm sudden grasp of Spring;
Like a woman when her lover has suddenly, swiftly taken her.
I hear the secret rustle of the little leaves,
Waiting to be born.
The air is a wind of love
From the wings of eagles mating—
O eagles, my sky is dark with your wings!
The hills and the waters pity me,
The pine-trees reproach me.
The little moss whispers under my feet,
"Son of Earth, Brother,
Why comest thou hither alone?"

Oh, the wolf has his mate on the mountain—
Where art thou, Spring-daughter?
I tremble with love as the reeds by the river,
I burn as the dusk in the red-tented west,
I call thee aloud as the deer calls the doe,
I await thee as hills wait the morning,
I desire thee as eagles the storm;
I yearn to thy breast as night to the sea,
I claim thee as the silence claims the stars.
O Earth, Earth, great Earth,
Mate of God and mother of me,

Say, where is she, the Bearer of Morning,
My Bringer of Song?
Love in me waits to be born,
Where is She, the woman?

SONG OF WHIP-PLAITING

In the dawn I gathered cedar-boughs
For the plaiting of thy whip.
They were wet with sweet drops;
They still thought of the night.

All alone I shredded cedar-boughs,
Green boughs in the pale light,
Where the morning meets the sea,
And the great mountain stops.
Earth was very still.

I heard no sound but the whisper of my knife,
My black flint knife.
It whispered among the white strands of the cedar,
Whispered in parting the sweet cords for thy whip.
O sweet-smelling juice of cedar—
Life-ooze of love!
My knife drips:
Its whisper is the only sound in all the world!

Finer than young sea-lions' hairs
Are my cedar-strands:
They are fine as little roots deep down.
(O little roots of cedar
Far, far under the bosom of Tsa-Kumts!—
They have plaited her through with love.)
Now, into my love-gift
Closely, strongly, I will weave them—
Little strands of pain!

Since I saw thee
Standing with thy torch in my doorway,
Their little roots are deep in me.

        In the dawn I gathered cedar-boughs:
Sweet, sweet was their odor,
They were wet with tears.
The sweetness will not leave my hands,
No, not in salt sea-washings:
Tears will not wash away sweetness.
I shall have sweet hands for thy service.

        (Ah—sometimes—thou wilt be gentle?
Little roots of pain are deep, deep in me
Since I saw thee standing in my doorway.)

        I have quenched thy torch—
I have plaited thy whip.
I am thy Woman!

SONG OF THE YOUNG MOTHER

        M'-m'-m'-m'-n! N'-n'-n'-n'-m!
Ai-i-he-i—ah-o-he-a-i-ne—
Swing my chiefling fragrantly
On the cedar-branch.
Cedar, Cedar, tenderly
Sway to the singing wind.
Bright flying Wind with song in thy white throat,
And light in thy wide sea-eyes,
The sky's blue feathers on thy wing—
Oh blow, blow, gently, softly, Wind,
Rock my chiefling, Wind,
In his little woven cradle.
In the dusk my fingers still threaded,
Needing no light.

I remember my mother sat near me often, watching;
Sometimes weeping. Yes, she wept;
Yet answered not when I asked wherefor.
In the night thou hast waked me at his side—
Dancing, in thy dark house, to the doors that soon must open
On thy white shining dawn-shores of life:
And I have seen the Moon-Woman's round face
Laughing through the smoke-hole, mocking,
Pointing to thy empty cradle hanging.
Ai! but her smile grew kind! She said,
"Wait a little longer, impatient one;
When next my round face peeps through the smoke-hole,
I will seek him at your breast."
Ai-i-hi! Very precious is the man-child!
Ere it is born a woman loves it.
How cam'st thou here, little Chiefling?
A woman gave thee life!

      Yes—my mother wept, watching me weave for
  thee . . .
And I have wept, too, a little.

      Strange, that pain came with love;
I knew it not until thy father sought me.
Yet—what woman would cast love out?

      Gladly in the dusk I waited him—
None told me, not my mother even, of the pang.
So my heart, joyous, sounded a song of drums,
Beating the loud wild march for his swift-trampling feet.
The breasts of love were as the eaves of a house,
Jutting through the red mists and the dusk of ending day,
Calling the hunter to enter to his rest.
The door trembled with strange winds—
He circled my house with the arms of strength,
And took me with weapons . . . Joy?
Ay. Yet I cried from the depths with a sudden deep cry,

And in grieving earth was the torch quenched.
... Darkness ... and his, his utterly, in that dark ...
None had told me ...
Nor that his strength would leap, rejoicing at my cry.

At dawn—it is our custom—I went forth alone
Into the mists that wrap the sleeping cedars
And droop to the pale unwakened sea.
Alone on the dawn's white rim I gathered cedar-boughs.
My tears fell, shining among the earth's bright drops;
For now I knew
Why the maiden plaits a whip of cedar-fibre,
To give into her husband's hand on her marriage-day.
Once I asked my father—it seemed so strange
A maid should weave and weave a rod for her own sorrow.
He laughed and said: "It is our custom; ay, an old custom—
I know not if it means aught now,
Or ever did have meaning."
My mother sat near. Ay, I have remembered that she spoke
    not;
But, silently, in the shadow of his body, drooped her head.

Ay, 'tis old, the custom,
Old as earth is old;
Ancient as passion,
Pitiless as passion—
Ay, pitiless, pitiless, the earth-way for women!
Bitter it is, as the taste of bright sea-water,
That he, who takes the gift, and wields our weaving of desire,
Knows not the meaning of the gift—nor can know ever!
Into the heedless hand of passion
We yield our power-of-pain ...
It is the law of the earth-way.

So it is with birth-giving.
Aii-he! the mightier pang,
The mightier loving!

And thou and thy father, the two Strong Ones,
Glad, glad of the woman's pain-cry!

   M'-m'-m'-m'-n—Ai-i-he-i—
Sleepest thou, little Fatling?
Ay, thou didst long drink at my breast—
(But hast not drained it of love.)
Cedar, Cedar, carefully
Guard my little brown cone
On thy earth-bending branch.
M'-m'-m'-m'-n—Ai-i-he-i—
Little life-bud on the bough!
Sleep, sleep, thou drowsy one—
Thou art guarded well.
Ay, rock, rock, safely, safely, little Man-Child—
A woman watches thee.

SONG OF BASKET-WEAVING

Kulasgh, Kulasgh, my mother,*
I sit at thy knee
Weaving my basket of grasses,
Weaving for my harvest of berries when the Ripe Days come.
Thy fingers gently touch my hair with fragrance,
Thy mouth drips a song, for the wind has kissed it—
(Love sings in thy mouth!)
The soil listens and answers;
I feel a stirring beneath me and hear buds opening,
The river chants thy song and the clouds dance to it.
Tonight the stars will float upon thy singing breath,
Gleaming like slanting flocks above the sea.
All the earth sings: and its voices are one song!

---

*Kulasgh, Cedar tree, considered the source of life by the British Colum-
bian Coast tribes, as it supplies all their necessities, even food in fish fam-
ine.

I alone am silent: I alone, a maid waiting him, the Fate,
The Stirring One, the Planter of the Harvest,
The Basket-Filler.
Kulasgh, Kulasgh, Mother!
See how beautiful, how liberal, is my basket,
How tightly woven for the waters of Love,
How soft for the treading of children's feet,
How strong to bear them up!
Kulasgh, Kulasgh, Mother, remember me—
Ere the Sunset and the Dropping Leaf!

THE CHANGE-SONG

Death's first snows are drifting on my cheek,
Pale are my lips
As the kiss of Cin-Uza;
I lie low and still.
Near me crouch my silent kinsmen,
They hold the breath and wait the hour of wailing;
They have wrapped the scarlet mourning blanket
Round the shoulders of the oldest man;
He has taken their sorrow.
He droops at my door
Like a bleeding hawk where the eagles have battled.
He is so old he feels not any grief,
His heart is cold,
In his ears no sound is,
And in his eyes no light.
Therefore have my kinsmen given him their griefs—
Because the dawn leaps clear into their eyes,
Because the sound of women's feet
Rustling on the cedar mats when the torch is blown
Calls sweetly to their ears,
And their hearts are beating for the hunt.
They may not bear the sorrow of my passing,
We have known strong joys together!

I take your loves, my kinsmen,
I leave with you no griefs!
Sing, my kinsmen, when ye swing me
To the topmost branches of the cedar.
Sweet-smelling arms of cedar, reach for me,
Tenderly receive me,
Hold me in the Last Caress under open sky!
Sing, my kinsmen, when the oldest man
Takes his lone trail through the forest.
He will wear no mourning-blanket when he comes again
    tomorrow!
He will say, "Rejoice—
I have borne your grief afar,
I have buried it deep,
The place is not known."
The wind of your singing shall rock me
In the arms of my mother, the cedar.
Yet there is a sweeter song, my kinsmen;
It is the Change-Song of Supreme One.
I hear it now,
He chants it to my heart;
Because pale death has crossed my threshold, and has clasped
    my hand.
"Fear not," sings Supreme One;
"I am making pure, making pure,
I destroy not life,
I am Life-maker!"

    The oldest man has entered the forest.
Ah! Ah! my kinsmen are wailing;
They saw me depart with Death
Into the White Change.
But I go on—and on!
And I sing the Change-Song of Supreme One:
Ha- eohos la no-ya ai-a me la-la
Q' oalahag' i-h-e-e la-wo!

SONG OF THE FULL CATCH

Here's good wind, here's sweet wind,
Here's good wind and my woman calls me!
Straight she stands there by the pine-tree,
Faithful waits she by the cedar,
She will smile and reach her hands
When she sees my thousand salmon!
Here's good wind and my woman calls me.

Here's clear water, here's swift water,
Here's bright water and my woman waits me!
She will call me from the sea's mouth—
Sweet her pine-bed when the morning
Lights my canoe and the river ends!
Here's good wind, here's swift water,
Strong as love when my woman calls me!

SPRING TO THE EARTH-WITCH

PAI-IYA TO SWI-YA KWENEWESALS

My eyes I will not cover!
I am Pai-iya, stepping free on the goathills behind thy village.
Blue shadows and white mists, like flowers,
Lie deep in thy green forests.
Night lingers in thy hair;
Pools of starred dusk are thine eyes.
Thy speech is gray fog, impenetrable,
Shrouding the port of the crimson lure—
(The ships of the trusting one are broken.)
Oh, flower-red is thy girdle at morning and evening!
If it were loosened there would be a race of men,
And thou the harbor of a thousand wondering ships.
I have lifted dawn before me as a shield,
Swi-ya Kwen-e-we-sals!

The Raven pecks beside thy door;
On thy roof the Thunder-Bird claps his wings;
Thy smile darkles across the skies.
Thy smile is death—
My heart is the riven sea beneath.
If thy scarlet girdle were unknotted would it stem the sea of
    my wound?
Nay! Call not me with the wind blowing through thy
    garments!
I have bound the mountains to my feet,
Swi-ya Kwen-e-we-sals!

Last night I saw winged stars in flight
Circling o'er thy dwelling.
They swung at rest on the points of the shore pine—
Torches red-spanning the bay.
My wolves, at my call,
In long gray troops fled up from the forest.
They sphered in guard about me—sleeping on my shield
    poised on the four world-crags—
As darkened silver cloud-mists wind about the moon.
I have shepherded them into the canyon between us—
(But my eyes I will not cover!)
Wilt thou come, daring, among my fanged flocks,
Swi-ya Kwen-e-we-sals?

What is this warmth stealing to my height
Like footsteps of a strange desire?
Wave on wave of pink and gold breaks over the white;
The petals open, chirring,
As if they were feathers on the Song-bird's swelling
    throat.
My wolves, with heads hanging and fangs covered, slowly
    moving, moving,
Huddle in the valley like sky-shadows before rain.
Whose steps flow and ripple over the dark moss,
Parting the green walls of cedars,

Blossoming among my mating flocks?
Whence this unraveling of flame blown loose across the air?

My eyes I will not cover!
I have woven thongs of the mountain mists
And bound me to the morning star.
Between the cliffs of Night and Day, thou emergest!—
Thy sod-brown bosom, the mystical craving eyes above;
The yearning fragrance of thy closed hands,
The wild winds between thy feet,
And the rivers under thy girdle!
I have cast down the great shield of the dawn!
Come, redden its rim with me,
Swi-ya Kwen-e-we-sals!

CHIEF CAPILANO GREETS HIS NAMESAKE
AT DAWN

White Head of Waters, White Head of Light—
Capilano; Cla'h'ya.
White head of the Chief to thee lifts greeting.
I am hoar with years as thou, great Father;
My hair hangs like the dropping ice
Of thy highest hushed waters.
I have lived a hundred years at thy foot,
Singing the prayer of thanks for life:
"O Kia-Kunaë, Great Spirit One, Great Kind One,
I praise thee for life, I serve thee with living,
I bless thee that in kindness thou hast made the earth
And with love covered it.
Yea, by thy kindness, men and trees stand forth;
Silently, to me, speak they the speech of brothers.
For delights the little rivers come among the hills,
Shining with the smiles of women;
Ay, as the merry murmuring of many maidens

Are the rivers; swift and tender in their coming.
(Because thou art kind, Kunaë, thou madest women.)
It is the morn, Kunaë, I pray, I praise thee."
Ah!—how many hundred years hast thou prayed thus,
    Capilano?
With thee this day, Mountain-Father, I thank Kunaë for
    another dawn.
I am girt with blanket and rope of cedar-fibre;
In my ear is a ring of fine bark.
Thou art belted with innumerable pine-trees;
To thee they are smaller than feathers.
The sun is the cedar-ring in thine ear,
The long sea asleep is the spear in thy hand.
It is still, with pale lights on the distant blade,
Pointing at rest to islands beyond the dropping sky.
Thou art come forth, as a hunter, to the dawn,
Herding the antlered shadows down the forest slope.
Their swift fleeing hoofs strike fire from the beaten sandshores
    of morning,
And the black wraiths swoon upon the bright opening
    sea.
With blood of his proud throat crimsoning the eastern sky
The great Stag of the Dark in the van falls dying.

———

    Here was I chief ere the coming of the white man;
Now is his village spread from this sea beyond my sight.
His canoes are floating villages;
They go by with a great noise and a black smoke.
His deeds are mighty; they leap with roaring clouds and
    thunder-fires
Into the blue quiet morning and the white moon-sky.

———

    Yet have I heard no sound mightier
Than the sun shattering the night
On thy stone shoulder, Capilano.
Yet have I seen no sight more wonderful and fair

Than the coming of the light,
When Day, the silver-winged gull, down-swooping finds the
    sea.
Yet have I known no thing sweeter, stronger,
Than the smell of piney winds and blue rippling sea-water,
And the kindness of Kunaë-Kia, the living One,
Waking the heart of the old chief
To another dawn of life.

THE WILD WOMAN'S LULLABY

What shall I sing to thee, Babe on my back?
Song of the Eagle that mates with the storm!
Hi-i-ri-i-ki! Ri-eek!
The wild gale is weeping, driven before him
To his nest on the black lone mast of the night;
Swinging, swinging, far out, high out, over the sea!
Hi-i-ri-i-ki! Ri-eek!
Thy father is Eagle-Go-High, chief of thy tribe:
Fiercest in war, wisest in council, swiftest in
    hunting,
Harshest and fondest in the tent of his woman;
He is my mate!

What shall I sing to thee, Babe on my back!
Song of the wind that is wanton forever!
Fleeing forever, luring and weeping, laughing and leaping
    forever;
Calling forever—calling—for the chase of swift wings,
For the drive and the smite of wild wings,
For the fold of strong wings,
For the sleep in warm wings.
OO-o-roo-o-rrr-ufffff-oo! Thy mother is Storm-Dancer,
    daughter of Winds.
What art thou, Little Chiefling, babe of my heart?

The star that I plucked from the mast of the night,
When the wings of thy father outstrove me.
Hi-i-ri-i-ki! Ri-eek!
Eagle-Go-High, this is thy son,—
He falls asleep, smiling,
To the scream of thy nesting-call.
Hi-i-ri-i-ki! Ri-i-ki! Ri-eek!

INDIAN LOVER'S HYMN

Sea-Song and Storm-Song
And drums of the night,
Drums of love's footfall beating through the dark;
Wind of my pulse and a breaking tide,
And my cry the one note, the one note,
Piercing the sky like a star over thee
O See-Gooltha maq-ha-ten-tle,
See-Gooltha with the two high breasts!

I am come as a river between hills,
Meeting the sea among cliffs—
O Waters surging to Waters in the monotoned might of the
    war-chant,
With the sod sounding back,
And thy voice—! sweet to the hunter's ear
Is the shrill arrowed hawk before the wind!
O See-Gooltha maq-ha-ten-tle,
Thy kiss opens the dark
And the moon unfolds in thine eyes.

Thunders of breaking day—
Long foaming surf-lines of light
Sweep the morning beaches,
Blown by winds that march and sing:
Tall winds, with hunters' feet, swift and trackless,

Scattering the light from Kunaë's* eyes
And the laughter from his mouth—
Red is love's glory on the forest
As a slain moose.
O See-Gooltha maq-ha-ten-tle
I arise from thy heart,
My lips lift, from thy kiss,
Flame-bright wings of new desire spreading to the Sun.
Give thy hand and leap with me o'er thy threshold to the
    Good Ground!
Run with cool palm to palm pressed, breasts beating,
Thighs by fleet thighs flashing, down the white swaying
    shore.
Brown feet and crags and trampling pines,
Tread to the sound,
Of Sea-Song and Storm-Song
And Drums of the Dawn!

THE SONG OF THE HILLS

FROM THE YOKUT

BEING THE SONG OF A MAN AND A WOMAN WHO MIGHT HAVE LOVED

This is the song of the Hills
In the hour when they talk together,
When the alpen glow dies down in the west and leaves the
    heavens tender;
In the pure and shadowless hour
When the Mountains talk together;

"Fir tree leaneth to fir,
The wind-blown willows mingle;

_____
*Kunaë: Supreme One.

Clouds draw each to each, dissolve, depart, and renew one
    another;
But the strong Hills hold asunder.

"Had we been less we had loved;
We had stooped and been tender;

"But our hands are under the earth
For the travail of her harvests,
Upholding the rain-sleeked fields
And the long, brown, fruitful furrow.
Terror taketh the earth
When the Mountains move together.

"But ever as winds of Spring
Set the meadow grasses caressing,
And the coo-dove's call.
To the coo-dove's mate
Resounds in the oak-wood valleys,
We shall thrill with the brooding earth,
We shall turn, touch hands, and remember,
Had we been less, how much we had loved
How nobly we might have been tender."

NEITHER SPIRIT NOR BIRD
SHOSHONE LOVE SONG

Neither spirit nor bird;
That was my flute you heard
Last night by the River.
When you came with your wicker jar
Where the river drags the willows,
That was my flute you heard,
Wacoba, Wacoba,
Calling, Come to the willows!

Neither the wind nor a bird
Rustled the lupin blooms,
That was my blood you heard
Answer your garment's hem
Whispering through the grasses;
That was my blood you heard
By the wild rose under the willows.

That was no beast that stirred,
That was my heart you heard
Pacing to and fro
In the ambush of my desire,
To the music my flute let fall.
Wacoba, Wacoba,
That was my heart you heard
Leaping under the willows.

PRAYER TO THE MOUNTAIN SPIRIT
FROM THE NAVAJO

Lord of the Mountain,
Reared within the Mountain
Young Man, Chieftain,
Hear a young man's prayer!
Hear a prayer for cleanness.
Keeper of the strong rain,
Drumming on the mountain;
Lord of the small rain
That restores the earth in newness;
Keeper of the clean rain,
Hear a prayer for wholeness,

Young Man, Chieftain,
Hear a prayer for fleetness.

Keeper of the deer's way,
Reared among the eagles,
Clear my feet of slothness.
Keeper of the paths of men,
Hear a prayer for straightness.

Hear a prayer for courage.
Lord of the thin peaks,
Reared amid the thunders;
Keeper of the headlands
Holding up the harvest,
Keeper of the strong rocks
Hear a prayer for staunchness.

Young Man, Chieftain,
Spirit of the Mountain!

SONG FOR THE PASSING OF BEAUTIFUL
WOMEN
FROM THE PAIUTE

Go thy way in comeliness!
Strong sun across the sod doth make
Such quickening as thy countenance.

Pursue thy unguessed errand and pass by;
I am more worth for what thy passing wakes,
Great races in my loins to thee that cry!
My blood is redder for thy loveliness.
Prosper; be fair; pass by!

SONG OF A PASSIONATE LOVER
FROM THE YOKUT

Come not near my songs,
You who are not my lover,
Lest from out that ambush
Leaps my heart upon you!

When my songs are glowing
As an almond thicket
With the bloom upon it,
Lies my heart in ambush
All amid my singing;
Come not near my songs,
You who are not my lover!

Do not hear my songs,
You who are not my lover,
Over-sweet the heart is
Where my love has bruised it,
Breathe you not that fragrance,
You who are not my lover!
Do not stoop above my heart
With its languor on you,
Lest I should not know you
From my own belovèd,
Lest from out my singing
Leaps my heart upon you!

THE HEART'S FRIEND
SHOSHONE LOVE SONG

Fair is the white star of twilight,
And the sky clearer

At the day's end;
But she is fairer, and she is dearer
She, my heart's friend!

Fair is the white star of twilight,
And the moon roving
To the sky's end;
But she is fairer, better worth loving,
She, my heart's friend.

A SONG IN TIME OF DEPRESSION
FROM THE PAIUTE

Now all my singing Dreams are gone
But none knows where they are fled
Nor by what trail they have left me.

Return, O Dreams of my heart,
And sing in the summer twilight,
By the creek and the almond thicket
And the field that is bordered with lupins!

Now is my refuge to seek
In the hollow of friendly shoulders,
Since the singing is stopped in my pulse
And the earth and the sky refuse me;
Now must I hold by the eyes of a friend
When the high white stars are unfriendly.

Over sweet is the refuge of trusting;
Return and sing, O my Dreams,
In the dewy and palpitant pastures,
Till the love of living awakes
And the strength of the hills to uphold me.

ALONG THE SOUTH STAR TRAIL
TRIBAL SONGS FROM THE SOUTHWEST

THE TOM-TOM

Drum-beat, beat of drums,
Pebble-rattle in the gourd,
Pebble feet on drifting sand . . .
Drum-beat, beat of drums—
I have lost the wife-made robe of bearskin . . .
Take the prize—mine the loss.
Have I lost too the courage of the black bear—
His power, his thunder?
Lul-la-by,
Games' queer lullaby . . .
O robe of mine!—
O luck of mine!

Drum-beat, beat of drums,
Pebble-rattle in the gourd,
Coyote feet upon the plain . . .
Drum-beat, beat of drums—
Coyotes crushed the tender ham-string and the bone . . .
A bull-calf bawls, dies alone.
Where are the herds of buffalo and the hides,
The meat, the tepees?
Lul-la-by,
Man's dread lullaby . . .
O home of mine!
O life of mine!

Drum-beat, beat of drums,
Pebble-rattle in the gourd,
Horse-hoof beat upon the ground . . .
Drum-beat, beat of drums—
By Wounded Knee ye buried them, buried them—
Red men's flesh, their bones . . .

By Wounded Knee we buried them, buried them.
The songs we sung, the dreams . . .
Lul-la-by,
The white man's lullaby . . .
O race of mine!
O brothers mine!

      Drum-beat, beat of drums,
Pebble-rattle in the gourd,
Pulse-beat in the fever . . .
Drum-beat, beat of drums—
Famine drank from the gourd bottle, ate the gourd;
Left the skin, the bone.
She walked the pathway from the east, of the departed—
Left me forsaken, alone . . .
Lul-la-by,
Tiráwa's long lullaby . . .
O blood of mine!
O child of mine!

      Drum-beat, beat of drums,
Pebble-rattle in the gourd.
Still feet in the grave-mound . . .
Drum-beat, beat of drums—
The gourd-rattle handle leads to the sun and life;
Leaves clay, leaves cold.
A purple smoke arises from bowl to float on winds;
Leaves ashes—my ash . . .
Lul-la-by,
Death's sweet lullaby . . .
O flesh of mine!
O hands of mine!

      Drum-beat, beat of drums,
Pebble-rattle in the gourd,
Dream-feet in the yellow line . . .
Drum-beat, beat of drums—

One half the feather of Tiráwa's bird is white;
The other black—'tis night;
Tiráwa's song at night is morning star of dawn
Where dance dreams, in light . . .
Lul-la-by,
The spirit's lullaby . . .
O soul of mine!
O breath of mine!

      Drum-beat, beat of drums,
Pebble-rattle in the gourd,
Calves' feet in starry plains . . .
Drum-beat, beat of drums—
A sacred herd graze on tips of fair fresh flowers
In garden—Star of Evening's.
A bison drinks mixed all-waters, pure
From Spring; 'tis hers . . .
Lul-la-by,
All-Life's lullaby . . .
O land of mine!
O plains of mine!

      Drum-beat, beat of drums,
Pebble-rattle in the gourd,
Dance-feet 'round the sun . . .
Drum-beat, beat of drums—
By the sun see the dancing white men with the red—
By Wounded Knee, a post!
There they blend their songs together, brother-wise;
Here the post, the paint . . .
Lul-la-by,
The Nation's lullaby . . .
O race of mine!
O brothers mine!

      Drum-beat, beat of drums,
Pebble-rattle in the gourd,

Child feet in the hogan . . .
Drum-beat, beat of drums—
A child has taught her little spider pet to weave
Bead-work at my door;
A child has taught these dimming eyes to see
Thread-work, star-lit lodge . . .
Lul-la-by,
Love's own lullaby . . .
O hogan mine!
O hogan thine!

      Drum-beat, beat of drums,
Pebble-rattle in the gourd,
Soul-feet in trail of wind . . .
Drum-beat, beat of drums—
Hear the great sea-feet, beating on the flint-rock!
Drum-beat, beat of drum—
Hear the beat of distant feet on South Star Trail!
Drum-beat, beat of drum—
Ti-ra-wa!
Earth's great Ti-rá-wa.
O heart-beat thine!
O drum-beat thine!

SA-A NARAÏ

So I heard it commanded,
On the edge of the mesa,
By the sitter on the mesa,
In the season of falling leaves:

Count thou, my son, the lights on South Star Trail;
       Sa-a Naraï
Trust not time nor strength—they are twin liars;
       Sa-a Naraï
On track of birth-dance the mourners wail—

Sa-a Naraï
The Tribe moves on—count thou the fires.
Sa-a Naraï
Beads, a few in falling rain; grains in desert sand;
Sa-a Naraï
The door of night swings wide—it will not close.
Sa-a Naraï
Still room for beads, dying hills for land;
Sa-a Naraï
The door is open—the Soul Trail glows.
Sa-a Naraï
I counted my sheep but not the bones;
Sa-a Naraï
A woman vows and goes her way;
Sa-a Naraï
Dust-wedded wealth—the desert owns—
Sa-a Naraï
Tomorrow smiles, while sad is yesterday.
Sa-a Naraï
Feast on wit and beauty—pendants of bone—
Sa-a Naraï
The eye-strings tie two souls today.
Sa-a Naraï
Fill the earthen bowl—fill jar of stone—
Sa-a Naraï
Youth blooms fresh—spring has not gone;
Sa-a Naraï
Winter gathers, gathers fruit of spring shower;
Sa-a Naraï
The frost-chain shakes—a soul moves on.
Sa-a Naraï
I saw a cripple, I saw a thief.
Sa-a Naraï
Go, hoe your corn with shoulder-blade of deer.
Sa-a Naraï
Where blows a wind, there stirs a leaf;

Sa-a Naraï
A bone enghosts a hoe—greed your spear.
Sa-a Naraï
If Red Moccasin moans, who knows the way?
Sa-a Naraï
I am ashamed before that standing within me—
Sa-a Naraï
The spirit upward flies—it will not stay;
Sa-a Naraï
Follow soon, thou must, the Voice within thee.
Sa-a Naraï
Shagwakwa laughs—in black night sings—
Sa-a Naraï
Give me my mother's bones—unto me, dreams!
Sa-a Naraï
A puff to the gods whither blue smoke wings—
Sa-a Naraï
Smoke now with me—soon the yellow line gleams.
Sa-a Naraï
Eat thy mother's flesh—she is the corn:
Sa-a Naraï
Is there a stranger who is not thy brother?
Sa-a Naraï
The One Above sung life—lo, love was born!
Sa-a Naraï
Hast shared the gift of thy first mother?
Sa-a Naraï
A little puff—a little kernel—
Sa-a Naraï
The Tribe moves on—it will not stay.
Sa-a Naraï
A little play by the trail eternal—
Sa-a Naraï
A little puff—lo, the South Star Way . . .

So I heard it chanted.

ON THE WAR-PATH

Hey—ye!
Hey!
Hey—now go, gather, gather living arrows, gather!
Stand ye in the white dawn—
Crouch, spring, run!
Hey now, plume feather, feather—eagle flying feather—
Strike ye in the red dawn!
Crouch, spring, run!
Hey, now pray power of storm!
Hey, now pray lightning's bolt!
Hey, now pray power of flint!
Hey, now pray weather, weather—war-like stormy weather!
Slay ye in the yellow dawn—
Crouch, spring, run!
Hey, now go, gather, gather, bleeding bonnets gather—huh!

EARTH-MOTHER

O, ho, yo,
O, ho, yo,
To thee, my life,
To thee, my wife,
To thee, my mother—

Who are these the many-feeding?
Heaps of horns,
Hills of fur—
To thee, I come to partake of food,
My mother,
O, ho—

So say'th the spring,
So say'th the wing,
So say'th my mother—

Thus, it was I heard the feet beat—
My ear down,
On the ground—
Yea, I put my lips to thee and drank song,
My mother,
O, ho—

So cries the tree,
So cries the sea,
So cries my mother—

There, the word was overheard,
By the cactus
Standing lone—
Yea, by the cypress thou wilt teach me,
My mother,
O, ho—

So walks the light,
So walks the night,
So walks my mother—

Even unto the long black shadows,
Goeth the frail thing,
Evening star—
Whither thou goeth and thy smile go I,
My mother.
O, ho—

So broods the dark,
So broods the bark,
So broods my mother—

Beneath the bark-blanket were the little men—
The six-legged,
Painted black and red—

Unto thee will I hide me to sleep,
My mother,
O, ho—

To thee, O breath,
To thee, O death,
To thee, my mother—

I saw it, yea in a dream, I saw it—
My soul
Arise from sleep—
In the morning, thou wilt call me,
My mother.

O, ho, yo,
O, ho, yo,
To thee, O—
Yo.

FEAST OF WOLVES

Ho, oh-o-o
Come ye shades, shadows come
Ho, oh-o-o
Come ye shades, shadows come
Come ye shades, oh-o-o, ho, oh-o-o
Ye night ghosts and dance ye
What—dark!
Ho, oh-o-o
Come ye wolves, wolf-howls come
Ho, oh-o-o
Come ye wolves, wolf-howls come
Come ye wolves, oh-o-o, ho, oh-o-o
Ye singers merry feast ye
What—bark!
Ho, oh-o-o

Come ye crows, crow-bills come
Ho, oh-o-o
Come ye crows, crow-bills come
Come ye crows, oh-o-o, ho, oh-o-o
Ye black robes and flap ye
What—hark!
Ho, oh-o-o
Come ye bones, bone-grins come
Come ye bones, oh-o-o, ho, oh-o-o
What—stark!

LONE-DOG UNTO THE DELAWARES

Brothers—Lennapi,
Hear ye, come ye, all ye—
By south-way, east-way, shore-land place,
Men come,
Boats come,
Float fast,
Handsome.
Man-who-Paints, much-talker, he much-walked
Easterly, south also,
All-time stalked—
Friends they, he says,
Sun-rise men, sun-born men, east-coming;
Great things have, wonderful, thundering—
Yea, great things, hear we, from clam-clam-sea—
Hear ye—
White-bird boat, great eagle, floats up streams,
Man-carrying, house-bearing, much-fire gleams.
Friends they,
Say they,
Come ye, hear ye, all ye,
Brothers there, cousins there, Lennapi,
Turtle men, turkey men, wolf clan,

Let us running-friendly be,
Let us brother-hearted be,
Giver-brothers standing we,
Men with meat, men with hides, everyman,
Come ye, run ye, all ye.
From Branchy-river-place,
From Straightened-river-place,
From Great-falls-at,
From Shore-land-at,
Sassafras-land.
Many caves men,
Riding waves men,
All ye Wolves, Turtles, Lennapi—
Bring your gifts, laying them
At Clam-clam-sea.

LISTENING*

The noise of passing feet
On the prairie—
Is it men or gods
Who come out of the silence?

BUFFALO DANCE

Strike ye our land
With curved horns!
Now with cries
Bending our bodies,

---

*Miss Frances Densmore's literal translations from the Chippewa furnished the keynotes of this and the following five songs.   A. C. H.

Breathe fire upon us;
Now with feet
Trampling the earth,
Let your hoofs
Thunder over us!
Strike ye our land
With curved horns!

WHERE THE FIGHT WAS

In the place where the fight was
Across the river,
In the place where the fight was
Across the river:
A heavy load for a woman
To lift in her blanket,
A heavy load for a woman
To carry on her shoulder.
In the place where the fight was
Across the river,
In the place where the fight was
Across the river:
The women go wailing
To gather the wounded,
The women go wailing
To pick up the dead.

THE WIND

The wind is carrying me round the sky;
The wind is carrying me round the sky.
My body is here in the valley—
The wind is carrying me round the sky.

COURTSHIP

When I go I will give you surely
What you will wear if you go with me;
A blanket of red and a bright girdle,
Two new moccasins and a silver necklace.
When I go I will give you surely
What you will wear if you go with me!

PARTING

Now I go, do not weep, woman—
Woman, do not weep;
Though I go from you to die,
We shall both lie down
At the foot of the hill, and sleep.

Now I go, do not weep, woman—
Woman, do not weep;
Earth is our mother and our tent the sky.
Though I go from you to die,
We shall both lie down
At the foot of the hill, and sleep.

THE LOST LAGOON

It is dusk on the Lost Lagoon,
And we two dreaming the dusk away,
Beneath the drift of a twilight gray—
Beneath the drowse of an ending day
And the curve of a golden moon.

It is dark on the Lost Lagoon,
And gone are the depths of haunting blue,

The grouping gulls, and the old canoe,
The singing firs, and the dusk and—you,
And gone is the golden moon.

O lure of the Lost Lagoon—
I dream tonight that my paddle blurs
The purple shade where the seaweed stirs—
I hear the call of the singing firs
In the hush of the golden moon.

THE SONG MY PADDLE SINGS

West wind, blow from your prairie nest,
Blow from the mountains, blow from the west.
The sail is idle, the sailor too;
O! wind of the west, we wait for you.
Blow, blow!
I have wooed you so,
But never a favor you bestow.
You rock your cradle the hills between,
But scorn to notice my white lateen.

I stow the sail, unship the mast:
I wooed you long but my wooing's past;
My paddle will lull you into rest.
O! drowsy wind of the drowsy west,
Sleep, sleep,
By your mountain steep,
Or down where the prairie grasses sweep!
Now fold in slumber your laggard wings,
For soft is the song my paddle sings.

August is laughing across the sky,
Laughing while paddle, canoe and I,
Drift, drift,

Where the hills uplift
On either side of the current swift.
The river rolls in its rocky bed;
My paddle is plying its way ahead;
Dip, dip,
While the waters flip
In foam as over their breast we slip.

And oh, the river runs swifter now;
The eddies circle about my bow.
Swirl, swirl!
How the ripples curl
In many a dangerous pool awhirl!

And forward far the rapids roar,
Fretting their margin for evermore.
Dash, dash,
With a mighty crash,
They seethe, and boil, and bound, and splash.

Be strong, O paddle! be brave, canoe!
The reckless waves you must plunge into.
Reel, reel.
On your trembling keel,
But never a fear my craft will feel.

We've raced the rapid, we're far ahead!
The river slips through its silent bed.
Sway, sway,
As bubbles spray
And fall in tinkling tunes away.
And up on the hills against the sky,
A fir tree rocking its lullaby,
Swings, swings,
Its emerald wings,
Swelling the song that my paddle sings.

PLEM-SALIA-KWI

AUTUMN DAWN

Plem-Salia-Kwi is the Hunter returning with plenty,
And the Fisher from the green sea.
His shoulders are heavy with deer's meat;
His great canoe is slow with salmon.
We listen to the nudge of its tall ghost-prow
In all our landing coves.
We hear the ground-wind of his moccasins
Rustling the forest-floors:
Swifter than joy they speed on the purple paths of the Fall—
Paths stained with fruitage, oozing odors.
He comes to us, his little brown blood-brothers by the sea:—
Through the dark silver-blue spruces, and the massed sea-green
     cedars,
Through the brown and crimson maples,
And the cottonwoods' dropping gold;
Through the pearl shimmer of the naked birches.
Plem-Salia-Kwi's blanket is the white, broidered, mist;
Its fringes are dew-bells
That tinkle little whispers down the mountain.
While he still slept,
Lake-Woman, Mother of Waters, wove him his blanket:
Wove it of the wool of the mist-herds
Drifting down from the cloud-ranges.
She patterned it in bead-drops, sun-colored—
A rainbow starts in the heart of each—
With blue ravelings from sky-patches,
With pink shells from the beaches of morning.
He bears the strong bent bow of the hills,
And the swift wind-arrows scarlet-shafted with dawn:
And the tall spear of falling light,
October light, the mystical weapon.
[Ah-h! Ahi! Ah-h! We sing to Kunaë
For the beauty and harvest of Plem-Salia-Kwi.]

The little children,
In laughing, leaping, running, stumbling,
Pattering and creeping down to the beaches,
Give thanks for the harvest of sweet, dried berries
And the plenty of the breast.
They go down to converse with the swallows,
Who bathe in the small leaf-locked pools.
Ak-hi! the shrill joy of the children,
At the twirring and flashing of brown wings in bright water,
And the twittering of news from all the nests of the sea-coast!

The pine-logs make a good smoke, blue, clear, sweet-smelling,
The cooking baskets bubble with water:
The women chant, while they heat stones for the baking,
Concerning the large baskets of food they have cooked,
And the racks of crimson, smoked salmon,
And the many trays of dried berries,
Sun-baked and jellied in long strips, packed in cool leaves.
They behold their men coming up from the caves
With hammers and copper, with silver and cunning shells;
And they clatter at their ears, saying:—
"Is not thy roof fragrant with cedar-trays of berries?
Have I not stored thy house full?
Hast thou not a little wayward son of thee at each of thy
    hands?
Is the cradle on my back—the cradle of thy despised little
    daughter—empty?
Where is another such wife?
Speak, O thou Hunter of Life,
That caughtest me unknowing in the pine shadows—
Ak-hi-i! Il-ak-il-ak!—
When I danced after Tem-Eyos-Kwi!"

The men answer not:
But in their eyes, behind their lashes, is a little smile,
Like light in the depths of a reedy pool.

Early, ere their clattering women woke,
They went down to the caves with their axes.
They have digged copper and silver and brilliant shells
From a secret store.
Tink-tonk, tink-tonk, tink-tonk!
Through the forest rings the song of their hammers.
The silent men are hammering rings for their women:
Rings, bracelets, anklets, for their women,
Glad gifts for their women, their mates.

For the silent men have seen
That Plem-Salia-Kwi walks not alone.
Through all his paths She follows him—his Woman, his Mate—
Sharing his blanket.
She has no other garment, her breast is bare,
She has given all to him she follows;
So comes he with plenty!
He tires not forever on his leagues of march,
Because her feet are set to his foot-prints,
And the gleam of her bare hand slants across his shoulder.
Therefore the silent men, the Hunters and Providers of Life,
Greet Plem-Salia-Kwi, the Harvest-Bringer, their Blood-
    Brother the Mated One,
With the tink-tonk, tink-tonk, tink-tonk of bright hammers,
Shaping gifts for their women:
Ringing their thanksgiving song for full joys—
Full baskets, full cradles, the full arms of sleep.

RENDERED IN THE RHYTHMS
OF THE ORIGINALS, BY ALICE FLETCHER
WITH INTERPRETATIONS BY TAHIRUSSAWICHI,
A PAWNEE

SONGS

FROM THE HAKO:

A PAWNEE CEREMONY

PREFATORY NOTE

The position of Tahirussawichi in the Pawnee tribe is that of a man worthy of respect—one versed in a knowledge of serious things, whose life has been devoted to the acquisition and maintenance of certain sacred rites. He is esteemed as a man of truth—one who has the favor of Tiráwa. He possesses a knowledge of curative roots, and often attends the sick, using herbs as medicine. He is the keeper of certain old and sacred objects, and leads in their attendant ceremonies. His great care in observing all the details of the intricate ceremony of the Hako is well known in the tribe, and much good fortune is believed to follow his leadership in this ceremony. His title is Kúrahus. This term is applied to a man of years who has been instructed in the meaning and use of sacred objects as well as their ceremonies. The word is sometimes employed as a synonym for a venerable man, one who commands respect, but throughout this paper it is used in its official sense—the leader of the ceremony.

NATURE OF THE CEREMONY

The teachings of the public ceremony were general in character. They emphasized, on the one hand, man's dependence on the supernatural for all the gifts of life, and on the other hand, his dependence on the family tie for the gifts of peace and happiness. The specific teachings were reserved for the Son. These began in the ritual to the Dawn (tenth ritual) on the morning of the second and third days, which prefigured the secret ceremonies of the fifth morning, when the bond of the family relation was extended beyond blood kinship through the symbolic rites which recognized the common source of life in Tiráwa atius.

Looking over the entire ceremony, it is interesting to note how older rites have had their share in the development of the Hako, and how the trend of thought among the native seers has borne them toward a conception of the brotherhood of man, a conception recognized as the noblest known to the human family.

This impressive ritual-drama may be compared to a medieval Miracle Play, and has exercised an influence no less profound on the tribes which have performed it. The chief persons in the drama are, the Father, the Son, the Children, and attendant Deities (the associates and representatives of Tiráwa atius, the Master of Life). Mother Corn, Kawas, the Eagle, the Morning Star, the Dawn, the Day and Father Sun. The Father is chosen from the tribe which presents the great spectacle; the Son is selected by the priests from another tribe by the curious psychic process described in the Second Ritual. Unusual blessings are supposed to accrue to those who take the leading parts.

THE HAKO: A PAWNEE CEREMONY

FIRST RITUAL

INVOKING THE POWERS

EXPLANATION BY THE KÚRAHUS, OR CHIEF PRIEST

At the creation of the world it was arranged that there should be lesser powers. Tiráwa atius, the mighty power, could not come near to man, could not be seen or felt by him, therefore lesser powers were permitted. They were to mediate between man and Tiráwa. The first song mentions some of these lesser powers in the order in which they come near to man, in the order of their creation.

INVOCATION TO THE GREAT SPIRITS

I

We heed as unto thee we call;
Oh, send to us thy potent aid!
Help us, Oh, holy place above!
We heed as unto thee we call.

II

We heed as unto thee we call;
Oh, send to us thy potent aid!
Help us, Hotoru, giver of breath!
We heed as unto thee we call.

III

We heed as unto thee we call;
Oh, send to us thy potent aid!
Help us, Shakuru, father of strength!
We heed as unto thee we call.

IV

We heed as unto thee we call;
Oh, send to us thy potent aid!
Help us, h'Uraru, mother of all!
We heed as unto thee we call.

PREPARING THE FEATHERED STEM

Blue is the color of the sky, the dwelling place of Tirawahut, that great circle of the powers which watch over man. As the man paints the stick blue we sing. We ask as we sing that life be given to this symbol of the dwelling place of Tiráwa.

We paint the groove red because the passageway is red through which man's breath comes and goes to give him life. The sun, too, is red, and the groove represents the straight path whereon the sun shines, the path which man must travel if he would live in peace and prosper. The teachings of this ceremony make a straight path along which if a man walks he will receive help from the powers.

I

Take we now the blue paint,
Touch with it the stem, putting on the sacred symbol,
Emblem of the clear sky,
Where dwell the gods, who, descending, bring us good gifts,
Gifts of life and plenty.

II

When the man begins to paint the stick green this song is sung.

Take we now the green paint,
Touch with it the stem, the mated stem,
Putting on the emblem, the sacred and living symbol.
Mother earth.
From above descending, bountiful blessings on thee,
Mother earth.

Oh, Kawas, come, with wings outspread in sunny skies!
Oh, Kawas, come, and bring us peace, thy gentle peace!
Oh, Kawas, come, and give new life to us who pray!

In this ceremony the brown eagle is called Kawas. This eagle
has been made holy by being sacrificed to Tiráwa. Its feathers
are tied upon the stem that has been painted blue to represent
the sky.

This stem was the first one painted and decorated, because
it is female and the leader. It represents the night, the moon,
the north, and stands for kindness and helpfulness. It will take
care of the people. It is the mother.

Throughout the ceremony the Kúrahus carries this feath-
ered stem.

SONG TO MOTHER CORN

Mother Corn knows all places and all that happens among men;
therefore the corn which comes from her must lead, must direct
us where to go.

I

Tiráwa, harken! Mighty one,
Above us in blue, silent sky!
We standing wait thy bidding here.
The Mother Corn standing waits,
Waits to serve thee here;
The Mother Corn stands waiting here.

II

Tiráwa, harken! Mighty one,
Above us in blue, silent sky!
We flying seek thy dwelling there.
The Mother Corn flying goes
Up to seek thee there;
The Mother Corn goes flying up.

III

Tiráwa, harken! Mighty one,
Above us in blue, silent sky!
Behold! We in thy dwelling stand.
The Mother Corn, standing there.
Leader she is made;
The Mother Corn is leader made.

IV

Tiráwa, harken! Mighty one,
Above us in blue, silent sky!
The downward path we take again.
The Mother Corn, leading us,
Doth thy symbol bear;
The Mother Corn with power leads.

Mother Corn having reached the blue dome where dwells the great circle of powers, Tirawahut, and having gained what she went for, tawitshpa, authority to lead in the ceremony, she descends to earth by the four paths.

SECOND RITUAL

PREFIGURING THE JOURNEY TO THE SON

The spirit of Mother Corn leads our spirits in the search for the Son. We draw near, in the spirit, to the village where the Son dwells. The Son does not see us as we stand there; he is sleeping. We fix our minds upon Mother Corn and upon him; we think of the gifts we are to bring him when we come to him with the Hako, the gifts that the birds and the animals that attend these sacred objects will surely bestow upon him—long life, children, and plenty. Now the spirit of Mother Corn touches him.

We fix our minds upon Mother Corn and upon the Son; if we are in earnest he will respond to her touch. He will not waken, he will not see her, but he will see in a dream that which her touch will bring to him, one of the birds that attend the Hako, for all the spirits of those birds are with Mother Corn and they do her bidding, and he may hear the bird call to him. Then, when he awakens, he will remember his dream, and as he thinks upon it, he will know that he has been chosen to be a Son, and that all the good things that come with the ceremony which will make him a Son are now promised to him.

CHANT OF THE MYSTIC JOURNEY

I

Mother Corn, Oh hear! Open our way!
Lo! As we draw near, let our souls touch thine
While we pray thee:
Children give to us. Mother Corn, hear!

II

Mother Corn, Oh hear! Open our way!
Lo! Our heads we bow, while our souls touch thine;
Then as one mind
Make the choice of Son. Mother Corn, hear!

III

Mother Corn, Oh hear! Open our way!
Lo! With head erect Mother stands, and then
Moves she through air
On her mission bent. Mother Corn, hear!

IV

Mother Corn, Oh hear! Open our way!
Lo! Now over hills, over streams, we go
Taking our way
Toward the Children's land. Mother Corn, hear!

V

Mother Corn, Oh hear! Open our way!
Lo! Our journey's end now is near, we look
O'er the strange land,
Seeking Children there! Mother Corn, hear!

VI

Mother Corn, Oh hear! Open our way!
Lo! Our eyes behold where they dwell. In their
Village we walk,
Seeking there the Son. Mother Corn, hear!

VII

Mother Corn, Oh hear! Open our way!
Lo! His lodge we find, through the door we pass.
Sleeping he lies,
Knows not we are there. Mother Corn, hear!

VIII

Mother Corn, Oh hear! Open our way!
Lo! Now at her touch comes a dream; then a
Bird calls, "My son!"
While his soul responds. Mother Corn, hear!

THIRD RITUAL

SENDING THE MESSENGERS

The four messengers are selected informally by the Father from among his near relatives. They are generally young men, lithe and strong of limb, and able to make a long journey quickly. The distance to be traveled varies from a few miles to a hundred or more, and as they must carry all their provisions, it becomes necessary for them to get over the ground as rapidly as possible.

The formal appointment of these messengers takes place in the lodge of the Father, in the presence of the sacred objects spread at ceremonial rest.

When the messengers arrive at the lodge of the Son, he sends for his kindred and consults with them. Only a recent death in his family or some catastrophe which has deprived him of his property will be accepted as sufficient excuse for his not receiving the Hako party. If he accepts the tobacco he will bid the messengers return to the Father and say, "I am ready." In either case he must make gifts to the messengers in recognition of the proffered honor.

THE FATHER'S MESSAGE TO THE SON

I

I bid you travel o'er the land to the Son,
And with you take these words of mine unto him:
"Behold! Your Father comes to you speedily."

II

We wait their journey o'er the land to the Son,
When they will give these words of mine unto him:
"Behold! Your Father comes to you speedily."

FOURTH RITUAL

VIVIFYING THE SACRED OBJECTS

On the morning of the day the journey is to begin the Kúrahus rises from his place in the lodge behind the Hako and goes outside. There he ties the sacred objects on the selected tent pole.

The rope of buffalo hair is used to tie these sacred objects to the pole, which is then set up at the entrance of the lodge. Here it stands where the wind of the dawn may breathe upon the Hako and the first rays of the sun strike the sacred objects and give them life.

SONG OF PRAISE TO MOTHER CORN

As we sing we think that Mother breathing forth life, who has come out of the past, has now started to lead us on the journey we are to take and to the fulfilment of our desire that children may be given us, that generations may not fail in the future, and that the tie may be made strong between the Father and the Son.

I

Mother with the life-giving power now comes,
Stepping out of far distant days she comes,
Days wherein to our fathers gave she food;
As to them, so now unto us she gives,
Thus she will to our children faithful be.
Mother with the life-giving power now comes!

II

Mother with the life-giving power is here.
Stepping out of far distant days she comes.
Now she forward moves, leading as we walk
Toward the future, where blessings she will give,
Gifts for which we have prayed granting to us.
Mother with the life-giving power is here!

THE HAKO PARTY PRESENTED TO THE POWERS

INVOCATION TO TIRÁWA

This song is addressed to Tiráwa atius. He is the father of all and all things come from him. We pray in our hearts as we sing. We ask Tiráwa to watch over the Kúrahus, to guide his acts and to guard his words so that he may make no mistake and the ceremony may be complete. From the east the flashes of the eyes of Tiráwa come darting through the air upon us and upon the sacred objects.

Look on us as here we are standing, raising our voices!
Look on us as here we, presenting, lift now these emblems
    that are so holy up to thy gaze!
Swift, a flash from out of the heavens
Falls on us as here we are standing, looking at thee.

INVOCATION TO THE GODS

The people are now looking toward the north, the moon, the night, the mother of the day.

We ask the powers of the north, they who can see the path of life, to lead us and make us able to walk, us and our children.

To all the powers of the east, west, south, and north we have sung and have presented ourselves. As we walked, we have traced upon the earth the figure of a man. This image that we have traced is from Tiráwa. It has gone around with us, and its feet are where we now stand; its feet are with our feet and will move with them as we now take four steps, bearing the sacred objects, in the presence of all the powers and begin our journey to the land of the Son.

I

Look down, West gods, look upon us! We gaze afar on your
    dwelling.
Look down while here we are standing, look down upon us,
    ye mighty!
Ye thunder gods, now behold us!
Ye lightning gods, now behold us!

Ye that bring life, now behold us!
Ye that bring death, now behold us!

II

Look down, South gods, look upon us! We gaze afar on your
    dwelling.
Look down while here we are standing, look down upon us,
    ye mighty!
Ye daylight gods, now behold us!
Ye sunshine gods, now behold us!
Ye increase gods, now behold us!
Ye plenty gods, now behold us.

III

Look down, North gods, look upon us! We gaze afar on your
    dwelling, look down upon us, ye mighty!
Ye darkness gods, now behold us!
Ye moonlight gods, now behold us!
Ye that direct, now behold us!
Ye that discern, now behold us!

FIFTH RITUAL

MOTHER CORN ASSERTS AUTHORITY

THE JOURNEY BEGINS

I

The mother leads and we follow on,
Her devious pathway before us lies.
She leads us as were our fathers led
Down through the ages.

II

The mother leads us and we follow on,
Her pathway straight, where a stage each day

We forward walk, as our fathers walked
Down through the ages.

Mother Corn, who led our spirits over the path we are now to travel, leads us again as we walk, in our bodies, over the land.

We speak of this path as devious, not merely because we must go over hills and through valleys and wind around gulches to reach the land of the Son, but because we are thinking of the way by which, through the Hako, we can make a man who is not of our blood a Son; a way which has come down to us from our far-away ancestors like a winding path.

CROSSING THE PRAIRIE

I

Looking o'er the prairie, naught our eyes discern there,
Wide the land stretches out before us;
Then we cry aloud to Mother Corn: "Doth thy pathway lie
    here?"

II

Heeding now our crying, while our eyes she opens,
Mother Corn moveth out before us
On the lonely prairie, where we see straight the pathway lies
    there!

SONG OF OBEDIENCE

Mother Corn speaks to us and we are assured in our spirits. The next song is to enforce obedience to Mother Corn.

I

Hark! She speaks, and quickly we turn to her,
Looking toward the west to the spot where we
Passed 'neath the eyes of gods; and now do we heed her
    words:
"Yonder is the place in the distant west
Whence I have come out of the past to you."

II

"Born of the earth and touched by the deep blue sky,
Have I been chosen by the gods to lead.
You are to hear my voice and follow my strict commands,
As your fathers did in the days gone by.
Thence come I to open your pathway here."

SONGS AND CEREMONIES OF THE WAY

The journey we are taking is for a sacred purpose, and as we are led by the supernatural power in Mother Corn we must address with song every object we meet, because Tiráwa is in all things. Everything we come to as we travel can give us help, and send help by us to the Children.

Trees are among the lesser powers, and they are represented on the Hako which we carry, so when we see trees we must sing to them.

Trees grow along the banks of the streams; we can see them at a distance, like a long line, and we can see the river glistening in the sunlight in its length. We sing to the river, and when we come nearer and see the water and hear it rippling, then we sing to the water, the water that ripples as it runs.

SONG TO THE TREES AND STREAMS

I

Dark against the sky yonder distant line
Lies before us. Trees we see, long the line of trees,
Bending, swaying in the breeze.

II

Bright with flashing light yonder distant line
Runs before us, swiftly runs, swift the river runs,
Winding, flowing o'er the land.

III

Hark. Oh, hark. A sound, yonder distant sound
Comes to greet us, singing comes, soft the river's song,
Rippling gently 'neath the trees.

SONG WHEN CROSSING THE STREAMS

I

Behold, upon the river's brink we stand!
River we must cross;
Oh, Kawas, come! To thee we call. Oh, come, and thy
permission give
Into the stream to wade and forward go.

II

Behold, the water covers now our feet!
River we must cross;
Oh, Kawas, hear! To thee we call. Oh, come, and thy
permission give
On through the stream to pass and forward go.

SONG TO THE WIND

I

Hither, Winds, come to us, touch where water
O'er us flowed when we waded;
Come, oh, Winds, come!

II

Lo! The Winds round us sweep where water
O'er us flowed. Safe now are we,
By the Winds safe.

SONG TO THE MOUNTAINS

I

Mountains loom upon the path we take;
Yonder peak now rises sharp and clear;
Behold! It stands with its head uplifted,
Thither go we, since our way lies there.

II

Mountains loom upon the path we take;
Yonder peak now rises sharp and clear;
Behold! We climb, drawing near its summit;
Steeper grows the way and slow our steps.

III

Mountains loom upon the path we take;
Yonder peak that rises sharp and clear,
Behold us now on its head uplifted;
Planting there our feet, we stand secure.

IV

Mountains loom upon the path we take;
Yonder peak that rose so sharp and clear,
Behold us now on its head uplifted;
Resting there at last, we sing our song.

SONG TO THE MESA

I

The mesa see; its flat top like a straight line cuts across the
    sky;
It blocks our path, and we must climb, the mesa climb.

II

More mesas see; their flat tops rise against the sky, they bar
    our path;
We reach their base, and we must climb, the mesas climb.

III

The mesas' side we now ascend, the sharp ridge pass, its flat
    top reach;
There lies their base that we must take, and forward go.

IV

The mesas rise around us still, their flat tops cut across the
    sky:
They block our way, yet still we climb, the mesas climb.

MOTHER CORN REASSERTS LEADERSHIP

THE SEARCH FOR THE CHILDREN

I

Here we give our thanks, led by Mother Corn,
As our eyes dwell upon the borders of the land
Where dwell the Children we are seeking.

II

Now our eyes look on people walking to.
Soon our eyes catch the print of footsteps on the ground,
Made by the Children we are seeking.

III

Still we travel on, led by Mother Corn.
Now our eyes look on people walking to and fro;
They the Children are, we are seeking.

As we move on and enter the land of the Children we sing, in
the second stanza, about their footprints, the marks of their
moccasins where they have walked to and fro on the ground.

We may not actually see these marks, but the song repre-
sents us as seeing them; Mother Corn has seen them, and she is
leading us.

When the village of the Children is in sight the following

song is sung. Mother Corn speaks in the first stanza and tells us she has come again to this place. Her spirit had been here before when she came seeking the Son. To-day we have arrived with her at this her destination, and we give thanks to Mother Corn.

SONG OF THE JOURNEY'S END

I

Here is the place where I came, seeking to find the Son;
Here have I led you again, here is our journey's end.
Thanks we give unto the Mother Corn!
Here is the place where she came, seeking to find the Son;
Here she has led us again, here is our journey's end.

II

Here to this place have we come, bringing the Son our gifts,
All of the gifts that go forth bearing the promised help.
Thanks he'll give as he sees, Mother Corn,
All of the gifts that we bring, bring to his village here;
Here, where you led, Mother Corn; here, where our journey
    ends.

SIXTH RITUAL

THE SON'S MESSAGES RECEIVED

I

Now our eyes look on him who is here;
He is as the Son we have sought;
He brings again tidings from the Son:
"Father, come to me, here I sit,
Waiting here for thee."

II

Now our eyes look on him who is clad
As befits the Son we have sought;

He, arising, walks; follow we his steps,
Moving slowly on toward the Son,
Where he waiting sits.

The pack containing the clothing provided for this representative of the Son is now opened. After the messenger has finished eating he is dressed in the new clothing.

We clothe him because that is an act which marks the care of a father for his child. The garments we put upon him are fine and embroidered; these fine and carefully made garments show that we have been thinking of him, that we regard him highly and wish to do him honor.

Just before we reach the village we halt and sing the next song.

SEEKING THE SON

I

Where is he, the Son?
Where his dwelling place that I seek?
Which can be his lodge, where he sits
Silent, waiting, waiting there for me?

II

Here is he, the Son,
Here is his dwelling place that I seek;
This is here his lodge, where he sits
Silent, waiting, waiting here for me.

SEVENTH RITUAL

THE CONSECRATION OF THE LODGE

When the Son has dispatched his messenger to the Hako party, he with a few of his near relatives, enters the lodge set apart for the ceremony, there to await the return of his messenger and the coming of the Fathers.

He seats himself at the south side of the lodge near the door. This is the humblest place, and he takes it to show that he is not seeking his own honor. By the choice of him as the Son a very high honor has been bestowed upon him, and his appreciation of this is shown by his taking the seat of the lowliest and not assuming prominence before the people.

The Kúrahus directs the chief of the Hako party to advance one step and to stand upon the threshold while the first stanza of the next song is sung.

TOUCHING AND CROSSING THE THRESHOLD

I

Sent down by powers on high,
She bears a promise most sure;
The Mother Corn breathes forth life,
On threshold She stands
Of my Son's dwelling. All's well!

II

Sent down by powers on high,
She bears a promise most sure—
Now Kawas, bringing new life,
The threshold crosses
Of my Son's dwelling. All's well!

MOTHER CORN BREATHING LIFE IS NOW WALKING IN THE LODGE

I

The Mother Corn, with breath of life,
Now enters into my Son's lodge;
There she walks within:
With breath of life walks Mother Corn.
The Mother Corn, with breath of life,

Now circles she within the lodge,
Walking round within;
With breath of life walks Mother Corn.

KAWAS HOVERS OVERHEAD IN THE LODGE

I

Kawas, bearing new life, entereth this dwelling,
Comes as to her own nest, on her spread pinions;
There so gently she hovers over these her Children.

II

Kawas, bearing new life, flieth through this dwelling,
All the lodge she cleanses, with her wings sweeping,
Making clear the place, sweeping out the harm and danger.

CLOTHING THE SON AND OFFERING THE SMOKE

The lodge having been made ready as a nest within which life might be given and made secure, the Father performs his first act of recognition and responsibility. He puts upon the Son the garments he has previously prepared for the purpose. When clad in the finely embroidered clothing, the Son is told to make the offering of smoke to Tiráwa atius, as a prayer for the consecration of the new-born relationship.

THE SON PRAYS TO THE GODS

I

My son, now heed, attend to the command I give to you;
Oh, speak to the gods list'ning above us!
Oh, let your prayers ascend to the mighty ones on high!

II

My son obeys. His voice is now trav'ling far, speeding on;
It goes to the list'ning gods above us;
There will his prayer be heard by the mighty ones on high.

SONG OF THE PRAYER SMOKE

I

See the smoke pass by!
Rising high above, follows where his voice
Sped, intent to reach
Where the gods abide in the deep blue sky.
See the smoke pass by!

II

See the smoke ascend!
Now the odor mounts, follows where his voice
Sped, intent to reach
Where the gods abide. There the odor pleads,
Pleads to gain us help.

EIGHTH RITUAL (FIRST DAY)

THE FATHERS FEED THE CHILDREN

Now the heralds summon the people to the lodge and they
come, dressed in their best attire and bringing gifts.

IN PRAISE OF TIRÁWA

Father, unto thee we cry!
Father thou of gods and men;
Father thou of all we hear;
Father thou of all we see—
Father, unto thee we cry!

INVOCATION TO THE ALL-FATHER

When the Kúrahus begins to sing this song he must think what
this ceremony is for and be mindful that all the powers that the
heavens contain and all the powers that are felt over the earth
are now coming near and bending over the Hako.

All the powers that are in the heavens and all those that are upon the earth are derived from the mighty power, Tiráwa atius. He is the father of all things visible and invisible. He is the father of all the people, and perpetuates the life of the tribe through the gift of children. So we sing, your father, meaning the father of all people everywhere, the father of all things that we see and hear and feel.

> Father, thou above, father of the gods,
> They who can come near and touch us,
> Do thou bid them bring us help.
> Help we need. Father, hear us!

SONGS FOR LAYING DOWN THE FEATHERED STEMS

FIRST SONG

The feathered stems represent the eagle; the holy place, where the stems are laid to rest, represents the eagle's nest. A nest is made for the young; the making of a nest in the lodge of the Son by Kawas presages the fulfillment of the promise of children to the Son, as well as the establishment of a close bond, like that of father and son, between the members of two unrelated clans or tribes.

I

See where she comes to her little one lying so snugly and
    safely the nest in!
Hark! She is calling; hear her,
List as her nestlings make answer;
See how she gently hovers.
Happy our hearts as we look on her hovering over her
    nestlings so gently.

II

See where she comes to her little ones lying so snugly and
    safely the nest in!
Hark! She is calling; hear her,

List as her nestlings answer;
See her alighting gently.
Happy our hearts as we see her alighting there over her
    nestlings so gently.

SECOND SONG

I

Loud, loud the young eagles cry, cry, seeing their mother
    come;
Flies she to them slantwise, flies;
Then over the nest she hangs, there hovering, stays her flight;
Thanks, thanks as we look we give.

II

Thanks, thanks, from our hearts we give, thanks give as we
    watch the bird
As she to them slantwise flies:
Then over her nest she drops; there, folding her wings, she
    rests,
Rests safely within her nest.

NINTH RITUAL (FIRST NIGHT)

THE VISIONS ARE INVOKED

When the sun has set and it is dark and the stars are shining,
then the Children gather in the lodge. Some, as they come in,
will advance to the holy place and there drop a stick; this means
the gift of a pony. For every such gift the Kúrahus returns
thanks to the giver.

After all are seated, wood is piled upon the fire, and when
the flames leap high the Kúrahus rises, then his assistant and the
chief rise and the Hako are taken up.

The singers carrying the drum follow the Hako bearers as
they move slowly around the lodge, singing the following song.

I

Holy visions!
Hither come, we pray you, come unto us,
Bringing with you joy;
Come, oh, come to us, holy visions,
Bringing with you joy.

We sing about the visions which the birds on the feathered stems are to bring to the Children.

Visions come from above, they are sent by Tiráwa atius. The lesser powers come to us in visions. We receive help through the visions. All the promises which attend the Hako will be made good to us in this way.

Visions can come most readily at night; spirits travel better at that time. Now when we are met together we, the Fathers, call upon the visions to come to the Children.

II

Holy visions!
Near are they approaching, near to us here,
Bringing with them joy;
Nearer still they come—holy visions—
Bringing with them joy.

The visions have heard the call of the spirits of the birds upon the feathered stems, joined to the call of our spirits, and they are descending by the east from their dwelling place above, and are coming toward the lodge.

We sing, "They are coming," and the Children join in the song, as we pass around and wave the feathered stems.

III

Holy visions!
Lo! Before the doorway pause they, waiting,
Bearing gifts of joy;

Pausing there they wait—holy visions—
Bearing gifts of joy.

As we sing the visions touch and cross the threshold and then
pass down the long passageway leading into the lodge. As we
reach the west they have entered the lodge.

Kawas and all the birds have called these visions to bless the
Children. The visions have heard, they have traveled far, they
have reached the lodge, and now they have entered and are in
the presence of the Children.

IV

Holy visions!
Now they cross the threshold, gliding softly
Toward the space within;
Softly gliding on—holy visions—
Toward the space within.

V

Holy visions!
They the lodge are filling with their presence,
Fraught with hope and peace;
Filling all the lodge—holy visions
Fraught with hope and peace.

The visions which attend the Hako are now touching the Chil-
dren, touching them here and there and by their touch giving
them dreams, which will bring them health, strength, happiness,
and all good things.

VI

Holy visions!
Now they touch the children, gently touch them,
Giving dreams of joy;
Gently touch each one—holy visions—
Giving dreams of joy.

As we sing, the visions are walking away; they have done what they came to do; they are now leaving the lodge, and when we reach the west the space they had filled is empty.

We pause and we think of the visions going away over the silent earth to ascend to their dwelling place.

VII

Holy visions!
Ended now their mission, pass they outward,
Yet they leave us joy;
Pass they all from us—holy visions—
Yet they leave us joy.

VIII

Holy visions!
They, the sky ascending, reach their dwelling;
There they rest above;
They their dwelling reach—holy visions—
There they rest above.

TENTH RITUAL

THE BIRTH OF DAWN

As the night draws to a close, the Kúrahus orders the server to lift the skins which hang at the outer and inner doors of the long passageway of the lodge, and to go outside and watch for the first glimmer of light.

At the first indication of a change, when the air begins to stir, the server comes in with the tidings, and we rise, take up the Hako, and stand at the west, behind the holy place; there, looking toward the east, we sing this song. We sing it slowly and with reverent feeling, for it speaks of the mysterious and powerful act of Tiráwa atius in the birth of Dawn.

THE SUMMONS TO MOTHER CORN

I

Awake, Oh, Mother, from sleep!
Awake! The night is far spent;
The signs of dawn are now seen
In east, whence cometh new life.

We call to Mother Earth, who is represented by the ear of corn. She has been asleep and resting during the night. We ask her to awake, to move, to arise, for the signs of the dawn are seen in the east and the breath of the new life is here.

Mother Earth hears the call; she moves, she awakes, she arises, she feels the breath of the new-born Dawn. The leaves and the grass stir; all things move with the breath of the new day; everywhere life is renewed.

This is very mysterious; we are speaking of something very sacred, although it happens every day.

THE AWAKENING OF MOTHER CORN

II

The Mother wakens from sleep;
She wakes, for night is far spent;
The signs of dawn are now seen
In east, whence cometh new life.

The eagle soars where these powers dwell and can communicate with them. The new life of the new day is felt by these powers above as well as by Mother Earth below.

THE SUMMONS TO KAWAS, THE EAGLE

III

Awake, oh, Kawas, from sleep!
Awake! The night is far spent;
The signs of dawn are now seen
In east, whence cometh new life.

THE AWAKENING OF KAWAS

IV

Now Kawas wakens from sleep,
Awakes, for night is far spent;
The signs of dawn are now seen
In east, whence cometh new life.

H'Kawas hears the call and awakes. Now all the powers above
wake and stir, and all things below wake and stir; the breath of
new life is everywhere. With the signs in the east has come this
new life.

Kawas, the brown eagle, the messenger of the powers above,
now stands within the lodge and speaks. The Kúrahus hears his
voice as she tells him what the signs in the east mean.

She tells him that Tiráwa atius there moves upon Darkness,
the Night, and causes her to bring forth the Dawn. It is the
breath of the new-born Dawn, the child of Night and Tiráwa
atius, which is felt by all the powers and all things above and
below and which gives them new life for the new day.

V

Then Kawas stands and speaks forth:
"A child from Night is now born;
Tiráwa, father on high,
On Darkness moving, brings Dawn."

VI

"I understand now, I know
A child from Night has been born;
Tiráwa, father on high,
On Darkness moving, brings Dawn."

THE MORNING STAR AND THE NEW-BORN DAY

We sing this song slowly with reverent feeling, for we are sing-
ing of very sacred things.

The Morning Star is like a man; he is painted red all over; that is the color of life. He is clad in leggins and a robe is wrapped about him. On his head is a soft downy eagle's feather, painted red. This feather represents the soft, light cloud that is high in the heavens, and the red is the touch of a ray of the coming sun. The soft, downy feather is the symbol of breath and life.

The star comes from a great distance, too far away for us to see the place where it starts. At first we can hardly see it; we lose sight of it, it is so far off; then we see it again, for it is coming steadily toward us all the time. We watch it approach; it comes nearer and nearer; its light grows brighter and brighter.

INVOCATION TO THE MORNING STAR

I

Oh, Morning Star, for thee we watch!
Dimly comes thy light from distant skies;
We see thee, then lost thou art.
Morning Star, thou bringest life to us.

II

Oh, Morning Star, thy form we see!
Clad in shining garments dost thou come,
Thy plume touched with rosy light.
Morning Star, thou now art vanishing.

INVOCATION TO DAWN

III

Oh, youthful Dawn, for thee we watch!
Dimly comes thy light from distant skies;
We see thee, then lost art thou.
Youthful Dawn, thou bringest life to us.

IV

Oh, youthful Dawn, we see thee come!
Brighter grows thy glowing light
As near, nearer thou dost come.
Youthful Dawn, thou now art vanishing.

As we sing this song the Morning Star comes still nearer and now we see him standing there in the heavens, a strong man shining brighter and brighter. The soft plume in his hair moves with the breath of the new day, and the ray of the sun touches it with color. As he stands there so bright, he is bringing us strength and new life.

As we look upon him he grows less bright, he is receding, going back to his dwelling place whence he came. We watch him vanishing, passing out of our sight. He has left with us the gift of life which Tiráwa atius sent him to bestow.

As we stand, looking through the long passageway of the lodge, watching and singing, we see the Dawn come nearer and nearer; its brightness fills the sky, the shadowy forms on the earth are becoming visible. As we watch, the Dawn, like the Morning Star, recedes. It is following the Star, going back to the place whence it came, to its birthplace.

The Day is close behind, advancing along the path of the Morning Star and, as we watch, the Dawn vanishes from our sight.

DAYLIGHT

We sing this song with loud voices, we are glad. We shout, "Daylight has come! Day is here!" The light is over the earth. As we look out through the door of the lodge we can see the trees, and all things stand out clearly in the light.

We call to the Children, we bid them awake and throw off the robes that covered their heads as they slept and let their eyes look out and behold the light of day, the day that has come, that is here.

SONG OF THE JOY OF DAY

I

Day is here! Day is here, is here!
Arise, my son, lift thine eyes. Day is here! Day is here, is
    here!
Day is here! Day is here, is here!
Look up, my son, and see the day. Day is here! Day is here, is
    here!
Day is here! Day is here, is here!

II

Lo, the deer! Lo, the deer, the deer
Comes from her covert of the night! Day is here! Day is here,
    is here!
Lo, the deer! Lo, the deer, the deer!
All creatures wake and see the light. Day is here! Day is here,
    is here!
Day is here! Day is here, is here!

ELEVENTH RITUAL

CHANT TO THE SUN

On this, the second day of the ceremony, we remember our
father the Sun. The sun comes directly from Tiráwa atius, and
whoever is touched by the first rays of the sun in the morning
receives new life and strength which have been brought straight
from the power above. The first rays of the sun are like a young
man, they have not yet spent their force or grown old, so, to
be touched by them is to receive an accession of strength.

All the time I am singing this song I remember the Sun, the
Moon, the Stars, the Corn; all these were made by Tiráwa atius,
and I ask them to give us success and plenty; success in hunting
and in war; plenty of food, of children, and of health. The Sun,
the Moon, the Stars, the Corn, are powerful.

We speak of the sun as Father breathing forth life (h'Aars), causing the earth to bring forth, making all things to grow. We think of the sun, which comes direct from Tiráwa atius, the father of life, and his ray (hukawi) as the bearer of this life. (You have seen this ray as it comes through a little hole or crack.) While we sing, this ray enters the door of the lodge to bring strength and power to all within.

The first four verses of this chant are sung in the morning; they follow the movements of the ray. When the spot has reached the floor we stop singing and do not begin again until the afternoon, so that our song can accompany the ray as it leaves the lodge, touches the hills, and finally returns to the sun.

I

Now behold; hither comes the ray of our father Sun; it cometh over all the land, passeth in the lodge, us to touch, and give us strength.

II

Now behold, where alights the ray of our father Sun; it touches lightly on the rim the place above the fire, whence the smoke ascends on high.

III

Now behold; softly creeps the ray of our father Sun; now o'er the rim it creeps to us, climbs down within the lodge; climbing down, it comes to us.

IV

Now behold; nearer comes the ray of our father Sun; it reaches now the floor and moves within the open space, walking there, the lodge about.

Later, when the sun is sinking in the west, the land is in shadow, only on the top of the hills toward the east can the spot, the sign of the ray's touch, be seen. Then we sing the stanza as we go around the lodge the third time.

The ray of Father Sun, who breathes forth life, is standing on the edge of the hills. We remember that in the morning it had stood on the edge of the opening in the roof of the lodge over the fireplace; now it stands on the edge of the hills that, like the walls of a lodge, inclose the land where the people dwell.

V

Now behold where has passed the ray of our father Sun; around the lodge the ray has passed and left its blessing there, touching us, each one of us.

VI

Now behold; softly climbs the ray of our father Sun; it upward climbs, and o'er the rim it passes from the place whence the smoke ascends on high.

VII

Now behold on the hills the ray of our father Sun; it lingers there as loath to go, while all the plain is dark. Now has gone the ray from us.

VIII

Now behold; lost to us the ray of our father Sun; beyond our sight the ray has gone, returning to the place whence it came to bring us strength.

CHANT OF THE EAGLES

This song likens the bustle and stir of the Hako party as it comes into the village to the flapping of the wings of a flock of birds as they come to a place and alight. It refers also to the birds represented on the feathered stems—the eagle, the duck, the woodpecker, and the owl. The noise of the wings of these birds is what is meant, for they are moving with the Fathers toward the Children.

THE WINGS OF THE MIGHTY

I

Hark, the sound of their wings! Mighty birds are here now
    alighting, bearing promised good.
Hark, the sound of their wings! Surely the Hako is coming.
    Children, forward bring your gifts.

II

Hark, the sound of their wings! Mighty birds are here now
    alighting, bearing promised good.
Hark, the sound of their wings! See! The Hako has come. We
    children forward bring our gifts.

TWELFTH RITUAL (SECOND NIGHT)

THE RITES CAME BY A VISION

FIRST SONG

Was it, we ask, in dreams that the Fathers saw
Clearly the Hako, wherewith I make you now
As my son,
My own begotten?
Was it in dreams they learned how to make you thus
My offspring?

Truly, in dreams it was that the Fathers saw
Clearly the Hako, wherewith I make you now
As my son,
My own begotten.
Truly, in dreams they learned how to make you thus
My offspring.

SECOND SONG

This is the teaching, this is the word sent
Down to us from our fathers:

All of the wise words, all of the good gifts,
Brought unto you as a Son,
Verily, through a dream all of these things,
All, by the east descended.
This is the teaching, this is the word sent
Down to us from our fathers:
All of the wise words, all of the good gifts,
Now brought to you as my Son,
Verily, as of old, all of these things,
All, by the east descended.

THIRD SONG—TO THE PLEIADES

Look as they rise, up rise
Over the line where sky meets the earth;
Pleiades!
Lo! They ascending, come to guide us,
Leading us safely, keeping us one;
Pleiades,
Us teach to be, like you, united.

FOURTH SONG—OF KATASHA, THE DWELLING PLACE OF THE VISIONS

I

Give heed. We tell of Katasha holy,
Whence the dreams come down, when draweth the night time
near;
Near the gods is their dwelling,
They who watch o'er men; all silently come they down.

II

Give heed! The bird of whom we are telling
Sends the dreams to us, when draweth the night time near;
Kawas, she that is sending
Holy visions, bringing, silently bringing peace.

III

Give heed! The birds of whom we are telling
Climb with dreams to us, when draweth the night time near;
Down the path they are climbing;
Where the gods to men are traveling come they down.

IV

They climb, these birds; a dream each is bringing;
Bear they dreams to us, when draweth the night time near;
Kawas—she that is sending
Down the birds with dreams; so faithful the Hako birds!

V

Then back they speed, the birds that were bringing
Down the dreams that come when draweth the night time
    near;
Birds and dreams are ascending
Where the gods are dwelling, watching there over men.

VI

Now this we know in truth—where are resting
Dreams that come to us when draweth the night time near;
True it is that he did see them;
In a vision saw he Katasha, where they dwell.

FIFTH SONG

I

Mother Corn! Mother Corn! We pray thee,
Be our leader, foes entrapping!
Trusting in thee, we wander far, yet we see no foe;
Food is gone, hope is dead within us.

II

Then in dreams Mother Corn spoke to me:
"I will lead you, foes entrapping!

"Testing your courage, far have I let you go astray;
"Rise, my child, follow me to vict'ry!"

SIXTH SONG

I

As I lay sleeping, as I lay dreaming,
Out of the distance came one advancing
One whom I ne'er had seen before, but when her voice
    addressed me, straightway I knew her—
Lo! 'Twas our Mother, she whom we know.

II

I rose from sleeping, my dream rememb'ring
Her words I pondered, words of our mother,
Then I asked of each one I met, Tell me, how far may her
    shrine be? When I found it
Sweet smoke I offered unto our Mother.

PART II

THE SACRED FEAST OF THE CORN TAKES PLACE

FIRST SONG—TO OUR FATHER SUN

Father, unto thee we cry;
Father thou of gods and men;
Father thou of all we hear;
Father thou of all we see;
Father, unto thee we cry.

SECOND SONG

Father! Thou above, father of the gods,
They who can come near and touch us,
Do thou bid them bring us help.
Help we need. Father, hear us!

THIRD SONG—TO OUR MOTHER EARTH

I

Behold! Our Mother Earth is lying here.
Behold! She giveth of her fruitfulness.
Truly, her power gives she us.
Give thanks to Mother Earth who lieth here.

II

Behold on Mother Earth the growing fields!
Behold the promise of her fruitfulness!
Truly, her power gives she us.
Give thanks to Mother Earth who lieth here.

III

Behold on Mother Earth the spreading trees!
Behold the promise of her fruitfulness!
Truly, her power gives she us.
Give thanks to Mother Earth who lieth here.

IV

We see on Mother Earth the running streams;
We see the promise of her fruitfulness.
Truly, her power gives she us.
Our thanks to Mother Earth who lieth here!

FOURTEENTH RITUAL (THIRD NIGHT)

INVOKING THE VISIONS OF THE ANCIENTS

I

Oh, come hither,
Holy dreams—Our fathers knew them—
Hither come to us!
Thanks we give unto them. They our message will hear,
Calling them to come.

II

This way come they,
Holy dreams—Our fathers knew them—
Come they now this way.
Thanks we give unto them. Coming now, they draw near,
Coming now this way.

III

They come nearer,
Holy dreams—Our fathers knew them—
Come they now this way.
Thanks we give unto them. On the threshold stand they,
Holy visions stand.

IV

Now then enter,
Holy dreams—Our fathers knew them—
Enter now the lodge.
Thanks we give unto them. Enter they the lodge now,
Enter now the lodge.

V

The Son they see,
Holy dreams—Our fathers knew them—
See him now within.
Thanks we give unto them. Entered now, they see him,
See the Son within.

VI

Now they hover,
Holy dreams—Our fathers knew them—
Hover us above.
Thanks we give unto them. Pausing here above us,
Hover they above.

VII

Now depart they,
Holy dreams—Our fathers knew them—
Now they go away.
Thanks we give unto them. They are passing from us,
Going from the lodge.

VIII

Above rest they,
Holy dreams—Our fathers knew them—
Rest they now above.
Thanks we give unto them. Where they rest we send thanks,
Thanks send far above.

THE FLOCKING OF THE BIRDS

In the early spring the birds lay their eggs in their nests, in the summer they rear their young, in the fall all the young ones are grown, the nests are deserted and the birds fly in flocks over the country. One can hear the fluttering of a startled flock, the birds suddenly rise and their wings make a noise like distant thunder. Everywhere the flocks are flying. In the fall it seems as though new life were put into the people as well as into the birds; there is much activity in coming and going.

When the eggs are hatched and the young are grown, the birds flock; the promise of young has been fulfilled. In this song, which we sing toward the close of the ceremony, we are thinking of the fulfilling of the promise given by the Hako, that children will be granted to the people, so that they may be many and strong, and we sing that the great flocks are coming.

I

All around the birds in flocks are flying;
Dipping, rising, circling, see them coming.
See, many birds are flocking here,
All about us now together coming.

II

Yonder see the birds in flocks come flying;
Dipping, rising, circling, see them gather.
Loud is the sound their winging makes,
Rushing come they on the trees alighting!

III

From the flock an eagle now comes flying;
Dipping, rising, circling, comes she hither.
Loud screams the eagle, flying swift.
As an eagle flies, her nestlings seeking.

IV

It is Kawas coming, Kawas flying;
Dipping rising, circling, she advances.
See! Nearer comes she, nearer comes.
Now, alighted, she her nest is making.

V

Yonder people like the birds are flocking,
See them circling, this side, that side coming.
Loud is the sound their moving makes,
As together come they, onward come they.

VI

Toward the lodge where sits the Son they hasten,
Bringing forward gifts with joyful shouting.
Hark! Now they like the eagle scream,
Glad of heart, as when her nest she seeth.

FIFTEENTH RITUAL

SONGS FOR THE SIXTEEN CIRCUITS OF THE LODGE

The life of man depends upon the earth (h'Atira). Tiráwa atius works through it. The kernel is planted within Mother Earth as she brings forth the ear of corn, even as children are begotten and born of women.

FIRST SONG

I

Look on her! She who sought far and near for a Son!
Look on her! She who led from afar unto you!

II

Thanks we give unto her who came here for a Son.
Thanks we give unto her who has led us to you.
Thanks we give, Mother Corn, breathing life on us all.

SECOND SONG

I

Rev'rent our hearts turn unto the one who brings to us
Long life and children, peace, and the gifts of strength and
    food.
Rev'rent our hearts turn unto our Mother Corn!

II

Rev'rent our hearts turn unto the source whence come to us
Long life and children, peace, and the gifts of strength and
    food,
Gifts from Tiráwa, sent through our Mother Corn.

THIRD SONG

I

O'er the prairie flits in ever widening circles the shadow of a
    bird about me as I walk;

Upward turn my eyes, Kawas looks upon me, she turns with
   flapping wings and far away she flies.

II

Round about a tree in ever widening circles an eagle flies,
   alertly watching o'er his nest;
Loudly whistles he, a challenge sending far, o'er the country
   wide it echoes there defying foes.

FOURTH SONG

I

Kawas flying where her nestlings now are crying; loudly cry
   they when they hear her wings;
Kawas flying, cry her children, as they hear her come.
'Tis Kawas who now homeward comes!
'Tis Kawas who now homeward comes!
Quickly flying as she hears her young ones in the nest.

II

Kawas flying, o'er us flying, we her nestlings cry for joy as
   now we see her come
Kawas flying! Glad our hearts as now we see her come.
'Tis Kawas brings us good gifts! 'Tis Kawas brings us good
   gifts!
Kawas brings gifts to us; we, like her nestlings, cry.

FIFTH SONG

I

Atira comes, she brings you life, she gives you joy; to her give
   thanks as she draws near.
Now in the lodge before our eyes Atira moves;
Look upon her who brings you life, who gives you joy. Oh,
   offer thanks to Mother Corn!

II

The Hako comes within the lodge, it walks within; let us give
    thanks as it draws near.
Now in the lodge with Mother Corn the Hako moves;
Thanks do we give for all the joy it brings to us, the children
    here, from realms above.

SIXTH SONG

I

I know not if the voice of man can reach to the sky;
I know not if the mighty one will hear as I pray;
I know not if the gifts I ask will all granted be;
I know not if the word of old we truly can hear;
I know not what will come to pass in our future days;
I hope that only good will come, my children, to you.

II

I now know that the voice of man can reach to the sky;
I now know that the mighty one has heard as I prayed;
I now know that the gifts I asked have all granted been;
I now know that the word of old we truly have heard;
I now know that Tiráwa harkens unto man's prayer;
I know that only good has come, my children, to you.

SIXTEENTH RITUAL
(FIFTH DAY, DAWN)

SEEKING THE CHILD

The child referred to is usually a little son or daughter of the
Son, the man who has received the Hako party. Upon this little
child we are to put the signs of the promises which Mother
Corn and Kawas bring, the promise of children, of increase, of
long life, of plenty. The signs of these promises are put upon
this little child, but they are not merely for that particular child

but for its generation, that the children already born may live, grow in strength, and in their turn increase so that the family and the tribe may continue.

FIRST SONG

With the dawn will I seek, seek my child,
Among the Children seek
One the gods shall here make;
My offspring, my own child.

SECOND SONG

I

Where is he, the Son?
Where his dwelling place that I seek?
Which can be his lodge, where he sits
Silent, waiting, waiting there for me?

II

Here is he, the Son,
Here his dwelling place that I seek;
This here is his lodge where he sits
Silent, waiting, waiting here for me.

SYMBOLIC INCEPTION

FIRST SONG

The ear of corn represents h'Uraru, Mother Earth who brings forth; the power which causes her to bring forth is from above, and the blue paint represents that power.

We hold the painted ear of corn toward the little child that the powers from above and from below may come near it.

Now our eyes look on him who is here;
He is as the Son we have sought;
He brings us again tidings of the Son:
"Father, come to me, here I sit
Waiting here for thee."

SIXTEENTH RITUAL—PART II

SECOND SONG

While we sing the third stanza, the Kúrahus touches the little child on the forehead with the ear of corn. The spirit of Mother Corn, with the power of Mother Earth, granted from above, has touched the child.

The touch means the promise of fruitfulness to the child and its generation.

I

Tiráwa, harken! Mighty one
Above us in blue, silent sky!
We standing wait thy bidding here;
The Mother Corn standing waits,
Waits to serve thee here;
The Mother Corn stands waiting here.

II

Tiráwa, harken! Mighty one
Above us in blue, silent sky!
We touch upon thy country fair;
The Mother Corn touches there
Upon the border land;
The Mother Corn is touching there.

III

Tiráwa harken! Mighty one
Above us in blue, silent sky!
The path we reach leads up to thee;
The Mother Corn enters there,
Upward takes her way;
The Mother Corn to thee ascends.

IV

Tiráwa, harken! Mighty one

Above us in blue, silent sky!
Behold! We in thy dwelling stand;
The Mother Corn, standing there,
Leader now is made;
The Mother Corn is leader made.

THIRD SONG

This song means that it is accomplished, that the child has been encompassed by the powers represented by the united stems. It is a promise of procreation.

I

Here stand we while upon Tiráwa now we wait;
Here Kawas stands, her mate with her is standing here;
They both are standing, waiting, bringing gifts with them.

II

We finished are, as on Tiráwa now we wait;
The task of Kawas with her mate accomplished is,
And all the work they came to do is finished now.

ACTION SYMBOLIZING LIFE

The child, surrounded by the creative forces, is urged to move, to arise as the first song is sung.

The four steps taken by the child represent the progress of life.

FIRST SONG

I am ready; come to me now, fearing nothing; come now to
me here.
Little one, come, come to me here; fearing nothing, come.

SECOND SONG

Stepping forward is my child, he forward steps, the four steps
takes and enters into life;
Forward stepping, four steps taking, enters into life.

THIRD SONG

Here we go singing, looking on the child Borne in his father's
    arms, he leading us; Follow me singing, looking on the
    child.

SEVENTEENTH RITUAL

TOUCHING THE CHILD

On the preceding night water was taken from a stream; this
water is now put into a bowl. Every detail of this act is sym-
bolic. The time when the water was obtained was night, the
mother of day; running water symbolizes the continuity of life,
one generation following another; the bowl which holds the
water resembles in its shape the dome of the sky, the abode of
the powers which bestow life.

    The child is touched with the water upon the head and face,
an invisible outline being made, which afterward is to become
distinct. The first touching with water, one of the lesser powers,
is to cleanse and give strength.

FIRST SONG

I

Give heed, my child, lift your eyes, behold the one who is
    standing here;
Behold, my child; waiting here to bring the gift of strength to
    you.
Give heed, my child. Look! Water waits to bring to you gift
    of strength.

II

Give heed, my child, lift your eyes, behold the one who has
    brought you strength
Behold, my child! Strength you have and finished is the task.
Give heed, my child. Look! Water now has brought to you
    gift of strength.

Water is for sustenance and the maintenance of health; it is
one of the great gifts of Tiráwa atius.
The white man speaks of a heavenly Father; we say Tiráwa
atius, the Father above, but we do not think of Tiráwa as
a person. We think of Tiráwa as in everything, as the
power which has arranged and thrown down from above
everything the man needs. What the power above, Tiráwa
atius, is like, no one knows, no one has been there.

ANOINTING THE CHILD

As we sing this song the old man makes the same lines upon
the face of the child as he made with the water and the brush
of grass. This is in recognition that the life which has been
sustained and nourished is now consecrated to Tiráwa atius, the
Father above, who gives life to all things.

I

Give heed, my child, lift your eyes, behold the one who is
standing here,
Behold, my child! waiting now to fit and set you here apart.
Give heed, my child. Look! Sacred ointment now is here come
to you.

II

Give heed, my child, lift your eyes, behold the one who has
holy made.
Behold, my child! You are set apart, and finished is the task.
Give heed, my child. Look! Sacred ointment now has set you
apart.

SECOND SONG

The grass of which the brush is made is gathered during a cer-
emony belonging to the Rain shrine. It represents Toharu, the
living covering of Mother Earth. The power which is in Toharu
gives food to man and the animals so that they can live and

become strong and able to perform the duties of life. This power represented by the brush of grass is now standing before the little child.

While we sing this song the old man touches the forehead of the child with the brush of grass. The power of Toharu has reached the child, has come in contact with it to impart the strength that comes from food.

I

Give heed, my child, lift your eyes, behold the one who is
    standing here;
Behold, my child! waiting here to bring the gift of food to
    you.
Give heed, my child. Look! Grass now waits to bring to you
    gift of food.

II

Give heed, my child, lift your eyes, behold the one who has
    brought you food.
Behold, my child! Food you have received, and finished is the
    task.
Give heed, my child. Look! Grass has now here brought you
    the gift of food.

PAINTING THE CHILD

FIRST SONG

The paint symbolizes the red clouds of the dawn, the coming of the new day, the rising sun, the vigor of life. The power of the new day, the new life, is now standing before the child.

As we sing this song the old man touches the forehead with the red paint. The vigor of life, the power of the touch of the sun, is now on the child.

I

Give heed, my child, lift your eyes, behold the one who is
    standing here,

Behold, my child! waiting to bring the gift of life to you.
Give heed, my child. Look! Red paint waits, the vigor of life
to bring.

II

Give heed, my child, lift your eyes, behold the one who has
brought you life.
Behold, my child. Life you have received and finished is the
task.
Give heed, my child. Look. Red paint leaves the vigor of life
with you.

SECOND SONG

Blue represents the sky, the place where Tiráwa atius dwells,
and with this blue paint we are to make upon the child a picture
of the face of Tiráwa atius. It is a mark of Tiráwa atius' accep-
tance of the consecrated child and a sign of his presence. The
symbol of the dwelling place of Tiráwa atius stands before the
child.

I

Give heed, my child, lift your eyes, behold the one who is
standing here,
Behold, my child! waiting here to make the sign of him above.
Give heed, my child. Look! Blue paint waits to bring to you
sign of him.

II

Give heed, my child, lift your eyes, behold the one who has
brought the sign,
Behold, my child! brought to you the sign. Accomplished now
the task.
Give heed, my child. Look! Blue paint now has left with you
sign of him.

PUTTING ON THE SYMBOLS

FIRST SONG

The down represents the high, light clouds (cirrus) in the blue of the sky; they are near the abode of Tiráwa atius.

The down is taken from under the wings of the white eagle. The white eagle is the mate of the brown eagle, and the child is the child of Kawas, the brown eagle. The down grew close to the heart of the eagle and moved as the eagle breathed. It represents the breath and life of the white eagle, the father of the child.

While we sing this song the old man opens his hand and lets the down fall upon the hair. The soft, white clouds near the abode of Tiráwa atius have dropped and covered the head of the child.

I

Give heed, my child, lift your eyes, behold the one who is
    standing here,
Behold, my child! waiting here to bring the sign of clouds
    above.
Give heed, my child. Look! Down of eagle waits with the sign
    of clouds.

II

Give heed, my child, lift your eyes, behold the one who has
    laid on you,
Behold, my child! sign of fleecy clouds that near Tiráwa float.
Give heed, my child. Look! Rests on you sign of the clouds
    above.

We sing in the fifth stanza that it is accomplished, the head of the consecrated child now rests in the soft, white clouds which float near the dwelling place of Tiráwa atius.

SECOND SONG

While we sing this song, the old man ties the downy feather on the child's hair. Tiráwa atius is now with the little child as the double feather waves over its head.

I

Give heed, my child, lift your eyes, behold the one who is
    standing here,
Behold, my child! waiting here to bring the last great gift to
    you.
Give heed, my child. Look! Waits to bring the emblem the
    Father sends.

II

Give heed, my child, lift your eyes, behold the one who has
    left on you,
Behold, my child! left on you Tiráwa's breathing sign.
Give heed, my child. Look! On you rests the emblem the
    Father sent.

Now we sing that all is accomplished. The child has been fully prepared, the sacred symbols put upon it, the powers from above have come, and Tiráwa atius breathes over it.

The child is now told to look into the bowl of water and behold its face. The running water symbolizes the passing on of generations, one following another. The little child looks on the water and sees its own likeness, as it will see that likeness in its children and children's children. The face of Tiráwa atius is there also, giving promise that the life of the child shall go on, as the waters flow over the land.

EIGHTEENTH RITUAL

FULFILLMENT PREFIGURED

MAKING THE NEST

The circle represents a nest, and is drawn by the toe because the eagle builds its nest with its claws. Although we are imitating the bird making its nest, there is another meaning to the action; we are thinking of Tiráwa making the world for the people to live in. If you go on a high hill and look around, you will see the sky touching the earth on every side, and within this circular inclosure the people live. So the circles we have made are not only nests, but they also represent the circle Tiráwa atius has made for the dwelling place of all the people. The circles also stand for the kinship group, the clan, and the tribe.

The down represents the light clouds near the dwelling place of Tiráwa—the dome of the sky over the dwelling place of the people—and it stands for the protection of Tiráwa.

SONG

Behold where two eagles come forth!
Now they soar high over head:
See where one flies, watching, flies, guarding he
His mate who has gone to her nest, dropping there;
'Tis Kawas who brings there new life.

SYMBOLIC FULFILMENT

The child represents the young generation, the continuation of life, and when it is put in the circle it typifies the bird laying its eggs.

SONG

Within the nest the child rests its little feet,
Awaiting there the gift sent by gods above;
Descending there to him comes the promised life.

THANK OFFERING

An offering of sweet smoke is made to Tiráwa; then all traces of the nest are obliterated, and the lodge is once more thrown open to the people.

NINETEENTH RITUAL

THE CALL TO THE CHILDREN

The purpose of the rite is recognized by the important place given to children in this part of the ceremony. The ponies presented to the Fathers are each led up by a little child; the acting out of a man's war-like deeds is to honor his child, and the little child with the black covering upon its head and the picture of Tiráwa upon its face receives, with the chief, the gifts as they are presented.

In every instance the child is the tie between the two groups, the Fathers and Children.

FIRST SONG

Harken! List! We are calling you. Come! Come! Children, come!
Come! We're ready and waiting, your Father's waiting. Come! Children, come!
Hear us calling, calling you! Children, come!
Children, come! Come hither!
Harken! List as we call you, call to the Children to come.

SECOND SONG

Ready and waiting, we call you, loud we call you, loudly call;
"Come to us, Children," call we loudly, call we long; Oh, come!
Come! Come! Come!
Hear us calling, calling, Children! Oh, come!
Hear us calling, come to us here! Come!

THIRD SONG

Look, where they come, see them, see them, young ones and
 old ones!
Look! Here they come, this way, that way flocking together.
Hither they come, shouting like eagles,
Shouting come.
Joyous, happy, gladly come they, gaily coming, coming hither.
See where they come, flocking like birds, shouting like eagles
As they come to the Fathers.

TWENTIETH RITUAL

BLESSING THE CHILD

When I sing this song I pray to Tiráwa to come down and touch
with his breath the symbol of his face and all the other symbols
on the little child. I pray with all my spirit that Tiráwa atius
will let the child grow up and become strong and find favor in
its life.

This is a very solemn act, because we believe that Tiráwa
atius, although not seen by us, sends down his breath as we
pray, calling on him to come.

As I sing this song here with you I can not help shedding
tears. I have never sung it before except as I stood looking upon
the little child and praying for it in my heart. There is no little
child here, but you are here writing all these things down that
they may not be lost and that our children may know what
their fathers believed and practiced in this ceremony. So, as I
sing, I am calling to Tiráwa atius to send down his breath upon
you, to give you strength and long life. I am praying for you
with all my spirit.

The purport of this song is hidden from the people, but this
is what it means: All that I have been doing to you, little child,
has been a prayer to call down the breath of Tiráwa atius to
give you long life and strength and to teach you that you belong
to him—that you are his child and not mine.

SONG

Breathe on him!
Breathe on him!
Life thou alone canst give to him.
Long life, we pray, Oh Father, give unto him!

INCIDENTAL RITUALS

I—COMFORTING THE CHILD

Long ago there lived a holy man who knew all the songs and the rites of this ceremony, and to him came a vision wherein he was taught how to bring comfort to a little child when, during the ceremony, it cried and could not be pacified. In this vision he was shown what he must do to bring comfort to the little child, and he heard the songs that he must sing. The songs which he heard have been handed down through many generations.

When during the ceremony a child cries and can not be comforted, the mother, or someone sent by her, can approach the Kúrahus who carries the brown-eagle stem and ask him to comfort and quiet the child. The Kúrahus must comply with this request, so he rises and stands before the holy place, takes up the feathered stem and sings this song, which tells the brown eagle, Kawas, that its baby is crying.

FIRST SONG

Kawas, harken; thy baby is crying!
It grieveth, wailing and weeping and crying so sore.
Ah! It cries, cryeth so sorely;
Kawas, hasten, thy little one cryeth so sore.

SECOND SONG

Father cometh, now he cometh;
See him, little one; hark! his footsteps!

With him, see! coming are the eagles,
All are coming now to thee.

THIRD SONG

I

Look, my child, who is coming unto you;
Look up, my little one, now your trouble goes away, away;
Look! Above you flies one who guards you,
Whose presence brings you joy. Now your sorrow has
    departed.

II

Ah, you look! See the eagles flying over you.
From up above they come, from the clear blue sky where
    Father dwells;
They to you this peace-bringing solace give.
A happy little child now is smiling here light hearted.

II—CHANGING A MAN'S NAME

If any man of the Son's party had achieved success in war, and
his achievements had been acknowledged by the people, he could
request the Son to have the ceremony of changing his name
performed.

This dramatic poem is in a rhythmic form impossible to
reproduce in English; neither is a literal translation adequate to
convey its meaning, since a single word sometimes represents a
complex action, to the understanding of which a knowledge of
the customs and beliefs of the tribe is essential. The terseness of
expression was also intended to close the meaning to the unini-
tiated, keeping it sacred from the common people. Although
the form of the following rhythmic rendition could not be de-
termined as heretofore by musical phrases, the English version
contains nothing which is not in the original text explained and
amplified by the Kúrahus.

The ritual is in three parts. The first gives a brief narration of the institution of the custom of changing the name in consequence of some new achievement. The second shows how the man was enabled to accomplish this act. It began with his lonely vigil and fast, when he cried to the powers for help. The scene then shifts to the circle of the lesser powers, who, in council, deliberate on the petition which makes its way to them and gains their consent. Then the Winds summon the messengers, and these, gathering at the lesser powers' command, are sent to earth to the man crying in lonely places, to grant his desire. This part closes with a few vivid words which set forth that only by the favor and help of the powers had the man been able to do the deed. The third deals with the man's names, the one to be discarded and the one now to be assumed.

Harken! 'Twas thus it came to pass:
> In ancient days, a Leader and his men
> Walked this wide earth, man's vast abode
> Roofed by the heavens, where dwell the gods.
> They reached a place, the spot no man can tell,
> Faced dangers dread, and vanquished them:
> Then, standing as if born anew to life
> Each warrior threw away the name
> That had been his ere yet these deeds were done.

Harken! The Leader and his men
> Made there the Vict'ry Song, and set the mark!
> Ye must o'ertake, if ye would be like them!

Harken! The Leader and his men
> Turned then toward home. Their Vict'ry Song
> Proclaimed them near; the village rose,
> Looked toward the hill, where on the top
> Stood the brave men singing their Song,
> Heralding thus the favor of the gods
> By which they had surpassed all former deeds,
> Made new their claim to be accounted men.

Harken! And whence, think ye, was borne
    Unto these men courage to dare,
    Strength to endure hardship and war?
    Mark well my words, as I reveal
    How the gods help man's feebleness.
    The Leader of these warriors was a man
    Given to prayer. Oft he went forth
    Seeking a place no one could find,
    There would he stand, and lift his voice
    Fraught with desire, that he might be
    Invincible, a bulwark 'gainst all foes
    Threat'ning his tribe, causing them fear.
    Nighttime and day this cry sped on,
    Traveling far, seeking to reach—
Harken! Those places far above—
Harken! Within the circle vast
    Where sit the gods, watching o'er men.

Harken! This poor man's prayer went on,
    Speeding afar into the blue
    Heavens above, reached there the place—
Harken! Where dwell the lesser gods—
Harken! And great Tiráwa, mightier than all!

Harken! It was because a god
    Received this prayer, considered it,
    Favored its plea, and passed it on
    To him whose place was next, in that grand ring,
    Who, in his turn received the prayer,
    Considered it, and sent it on—
Harken! Around that circle vast—
Harken! Where sit the gods above.

Harken! And thus it was the prayer
    Sent by this man won the consent
    Of all the gods. For each god in his place

Speaks out his thought, grants or rejects
Man's suppliant cry, asking for help;
But none can act until the Council grand
Comes to accord, thinks as one mind,
Has but one will, all must obey.
Harken! The Council gave consent—
Harken! And great Tiráwa, mightier than all.

Harken! To make their purpose known,
Succor and aid freely to give,
Heralds were called, called by the Winds;
Then in the west uprose the Clouds
Heavy and black, ladened with storm.
Slowly they climbed, dark'ning the skies;
While close on every side the Thunders marched
On their dread way, 'till all were come
To where the gods in stately Council sat
Waiting for them. Then, bade them go
Back to the earth, carrying aid
To him whose prayers had reached their circle vast.
This mandate given, the Thunders turned toward
earth,
Taking their course slantwise the sky.

Harken! Another followed hard—
Lightning broke forth out of the Cloud,
Zig-zag and dart, cleaving their way
Slantwise to earth, their goal to reach.

Harken! For these two were not all
That hastened to proclaim the gods' behest;
Swift on their wings, ranging the path,
Black breasts and red, yellow, and white,
Flying about, clearing the way
For those who bore the message of the gods
Granting the man courage to dare,

Strength to endure, power to stand
Invincible, a bulwark 'gainst all foes.

Harken! 'Twas thus it came to pass:
The Leader grasped the help sent by the gods;
Henceforth he walked steadfast and strong,
Leading his men through dangers drear,
Knowing that naught could strike at him
To whom the gods had promised victory.

Attend! Once more I change his name!

Harken! Rirutskatit, it was
We used to call him by, a name he won
Long days ago, marking an act
Well done by him, but now passed by.

Harken! Today all men shall say—

Harken! His act has lifted him
Where all his tribe behold a man
Clothed with new fame, strong in new strength,
Gained by his deeds, blessed by the gods.
Harken! Shakúru Wárukote shall he be called.

CONCLUSION

LAST WORDS OF TAHIRUSSAWICHI

I have done what has never been done before. I have given you all the songs of this ceremony and explained them to you. I never thought that I, of all my people, should be the one to give this ancient ceremony to be preserved, and I wonder over it as I sit here.

I think over my long life with its many experiences; of the

great number of Pawnees who have been with me in war, nearly all of whom have been killed in battle. I have been severely wounded many times—see this scar over my eye. I was with those who went to the Rocky Mountains to the Cheyennes, when so many soldiers were slain that their dead bodies lying there looked like a great blue blanket spread over the ground. When I think of all the people of my own tribe who have died during my lifetime and then of those in other tribes that have fallen by our hands, they are so many they make a vast cover over Mother Earth. I once walked with these prostrate forms. I did not fall but I passed on, wounded sometimes but not to death, until I am here to-day doing this thing, singing these sacred songs and telling you of these ancient rites of my people. It must be that I have been preserved for this purpose, otherwise I should be lying back there among the dead.

SONGS FROM

NORTH AND SOUTH

SONGS FROM NORTH AND SOUTH

These songs, translated by Frances Densmore, together with their music, are to be found in the following bulletins of the Bureau of American Ethnology, Smithsonian Institution: Mandan and Hidatsa, Bulletin 80; Teton Sioux, Bulletin 61; Northern Ute, Bulletin 75; Pawnee, Bulletin 93; Papago, Bulletin 90; Yuman and Yaqui, Bulletin 110. The Tule song, by the same author, is from the Smithsonian publication, "Music of the Tule Indians."

MANDAN AND HIDATSA

SONG TO THE RAVEN

Raven
     I am going to die—
     fly away.

EARTH ALWAYS ENDURES

Earth
     always
     endures.

HE STARED AT ME

My dear friend
   your husband,
   at me
   how he stared.
Will you throw him away?

YOU DID IT

You did it
   therefore
   you wept.

I CANNOT SLEEP

O
   to sleep
   to lie!
I think, if—
   but I cannot sleep.

SERENADE

O
   to be a man!

SHE WALKS ALONE

A certain maiden
   to the garden
   goes;
   lonely
   she walks.

WE MADE FIRE

Comrade,
     in the daytime when we made fire
     it was pleasant.
I understand women.

TETON SIOUX

SONG FOR FAIR WEATHER

    May the sun rise well;
       may the earth appear
       brightly shone upon!
    May the moon rise well;
       may the earth appear
       brightly shone upon!

SONG OF THE SACRED POLE

Father—
     all these he has made me own—
     the trees and the forests
     standing
     in their places.

NOON SONG

Where
    holy
    you behold,
    in the place where the sun rises
    holy
    may you behold.

Where
    holy
    you behold,
    in the place where the sun passes us in his course
    holy
    you behold.
Where
    goodness
    you behold,
    at the turning back of the sun
    goodness
    may you behold.

IN A SACRED MANNER I RETURN

Friends
    behold me,
    in a sacred manner
    I return.
You, tribe,
    behold me,
    in a sacred manner
    I return.
The nation sitting holy,
    friends,
    behold me,
    in a sacred manner
    I return.
You, tribe,
    behold me,
    in a sacred manner
    I return.

SONG OF CROW AND OWL

At midnight
   may I roam
   against the winds.
May I roam
   at night.
May I roam
   when the owl
   is hooting—
   may I roam.
At dawn
   may I roam
   against the winds.
May I roam
   at dawn.
May I roam
   when the crow
   is calling—
   may I roam.

WHERE THE WIND IS BLOWING

Where
   the wind
   is blowing,
   the wind is roaring.
   I stand
   westward.
The wind
   is blowing,
   the wind
   is roaring—
   I stand.

EVEN THE EAGLE DIES

Soldiers,
you fled.
Even the eagle dies.

A WOLF I CONSIDERED MYSELF

A wolf
I considered myself
but
I have eaten nothing,
therefore
from standing
I am tired out.
A wolf
I considered myself
but
the owls are hooting
and
the night I fear.

OWLS HOOT AT ME

Owls
hoot at me;
owls
hoot at me.
That is what
I hear in my life.

Wolves
howl at me;
wolves
howl at me.
That is what
I hear in my life.

I LOOK FOR HIM IN VAIN

As the young men go by
    I am looking for him.
It surprises me anew
    that he has gone.
It is something
    to which I can not be reconciled.

YOU SHOULD GIVE UP THE WARPATH

Going on the warpath
    you should give up,
    and you should desire
    to settle down
    and stop for good.

A PRAIRIE FIRE

A prairie fire
    I started
    when you were intent on women
    and hindered by them.
Did you see it?
    well,
    it was I
    who did it.

SONG OF SITTING BULL

A warrior
  I have been;
  now
  it is all over.
A hard time
  I have.

SONG OF THE FAMINE

The old men
  now are so few
  that they are not worth counting.
I myself am
  the last living,
  therefore
  a hard time
  I am having.

NORTHERN UTE

DANCE SONG

On a mountain
  the noise of the wind.

PAWNEE

UNREAL THE BUFFALO IS STANDING

He said, unreal the buffalo is standing.
These are his sayings,
    unreal the buffalo is standing,
    unreal he stands in the open space,
    unreal he is standing.

I AM LIKE A BEAR

I am like a bear.
I hold up my hands
    waiting for the sun to rise.

SPRING IS OPENING

Spring is opening.
I can smell the different perfumes
    of the white weeds used in the dance.

THE WHITE FOX

Yonder it comes.
The expanse of earth is wide.
My brother the fox spoke and said,
    "Behold and see the wideness of the earth,
    the white foxes know the earth is wide."

IT IS MINE, THIS COUNTRY WIDE

Yonder they are coming.
Although strange misfortunes have befallen me,
yet it is mine, this country wide.

THE THUNDER SPOKE QUIETLY

Beloved, it is good,
he is saying quietly,
the thunder, it is good.

OUR HEARTS ARE SET IN THE HEAVENS

It is there that our hearts are set,
in the expanse of the heavens.

THE HEAVENS ARE SPEAKING

I stood here, I stood there,
the clouds are speaking.
I say, "You are the ruling power,
I do not understand, I only know what I am told.
You are the ruling power, you are now speaking.
This power is yours, O heavens."

MAD CHIEF MOURNS FOR HIS GRANDSON

Mad chief sings as he walks,
    his spirit is glad as he walks.
Push-Forward is no longer among us,
    yet we seem to see him.
Yonder he comes.

PAPAGO

WHITE FEATHERS ALONG THE EDGE OF THE WORLD

Downy white feathers
    are moving beneath the sunset
    and along the edge of the world.

WHO IS GOING TO MARRY ME

Who are you, nice boys?
Who is going to marry me?

TERRIBLE IN ITS POWER

Hanging motionless in the sky
    yet terrible in its power to destroy.

THE MAN WHO HAS NO JOY

Who is the man who killed an enemy
and has no joy?
I am having all the joy alone.

THE WOMAN BY THE SEA SINGS

Where am I running from,
that I come here?
Am I crazy woman
with a painted face?

I MET A MEXICAN

While I was running I met a Mexican who said,
"How do you do?"
While I was running I met a Mexican with a long beard who
said,
"How do you do?"

THE BRIGHT MORNING

The bright morning begins to shine.
Get up, three of you, and see Manasi Mountain.
On top of it is yellow water.
I went there, drank the water, and staggered in running.

SINGING TO THE LEAVES AND FLOWERS

Crazy woman, crazy woman, trying to sing to mescal leaves,
how can she sing to them and make the wind come?
Young children, trying to sing to *bahwi* flowers,
how can they sing to *bahwi* flowers and bring rain?

SONG OF THE HORSE

Black hair rope is what you used in roping me.
You treated me badly.
You even threw me down and tied me.
Not satisfied with that, you tied a knot in my tail.
That made me disgusted.

SONG OF THE WHITE MOUNTAIN

A white mountain is far at the west.
It stands beautiful.
It has brilliant white arches of light
    bending down toward the earth.

THE LITTLE CAPTIVE CHILDREN

Men shouting "brother,"
    men shouting "brother."
Among the mountains they have
    taken little Apache children
    where the sun went down in sorrow.
All women,
    what shall we do to realize this?

A POOR MAN

A poor man takes the songs in his hand
    and drops them near the place where the sun sets.
See, Cowaka, run to them and take them in your hand
    and place them under the sunset.

THE WIND BLOWS FROM THE SEA

By the sandy water I breathe in the odor of the sea;
From there the wind comes and blows over the world.
By the sandy water I breathe in the odor of the sea;
From there the clouds come and rain falls over the world.

BEFORE STARTING ON THE WARPATH

I am going to walk far, far,
I hope to have a fine morning somewhere.
I am going to run far, far,
I hope to have a good night somewhere.

THE VOICE OF THE HERALD

When the morning starts and the sun comes up,
When the morning starts and the sun comes up,
At that time the voice of the herald sounds sweet.
It seems to be calling to me.

THE MORNING STAR

The morning star is up.
I cross the mountains.
into the light of the sea.

EVENING SONG

The sun is slowly departing,
It is slower in its setting;
Black bats will be swooping when the sun is gone,
That is all.

The spirit children are beneath,
They are moving back and forth;
They roll in play among tufts of white eagle down,
　That is all.

IN THE GREAT NIGHT

In the great night my heart will go out;
Toward me the darkness comes rustling.
In the great night my heart will go out.

WE SMOKE TOGETHER
SUNG BY AN APACHE SPIRIT

It was a sad thing you did;
It was a sad thing you did,
But now we smoke together.
The smoke will gather inside us.

RAIN SONGS

1

Clouds are standing in the east, they are approaching,
It rains in the distance;
Now it is raining here and the thunder rolls.

2

Green rock mountains are thundering with clouds.
With this thunder the Akim village is shaking.
The water will come down the arroyo
　　and I will float on the water.
Afterward the corn will ripen in the fields.

3

Close to the west the great ocean is singing.
The waves are rolling toward me, covered with many clouds.
Even here I catch the sound.
The earth is shaking beneath me and I hear deep rumbling.

4

A cloud on top of Evergreen Mountain is singing,
A cloud on top of Evergreen Mountain is standing still.
It is raining and thundering up there,
It is raining here.
Under the mountain the corn tassels are shaking,
Under the mountain the slender spikes of child corn
    are glistening.

YUMAN AND YAQUI
COLORADO RIVER BASIN

THE WATER BUG AND THE SHADOWS

The water bug
   is drawing
    the shadows of the evening
    toward him on the water.

THE DEER IS TAKING AWAY THE DAYLIGHT

The deer is taking away the daylight.
After taking away the daylight
   he named it Darkness.

SONG OF ADMIRATION

In Cocori is a young girl
    whose name is Hesucita.
She is a pretty girl,
    her eyes look like stars;
    her pretty eyes are like stars moving.

THE OWL HOOTED

The owl was requested
    to do as much as he knew how.
He only hooted and told of the morning star,
And hooted again and told of the dawn.

THE BUSH IS SINGING

The bush is sitting
    under a tree
    and singing.

THE RISING SUN

The sun is coming up.
It is time to go out
    and see the clouds.

THE DEER AND THE FLOWER

The deer
    looks at a flower.

SONG OF BROWN BUZZARD AFTER REMOVING HIS SCALP

You must enjoy yourselves in the evening.
Look at me. See how I look
and yet I am happy.

TULE
PANAMA

TULE LOVE SONG

Many pretty flowers, red, blue and yellow;
    we say to the girls, "Let us go and walk among the
flowers."
The wind comes and sways the flowers,
    the girls are like that when they dance;
    some are wide-open, large flowers and some are tiny
little flowers.
The birds love the sunshine and the starlight;
    the flowers smell sweet.
The girls are sweeter than the flowers.